A Go...

a look at leisure activities in Past Times

Bob McCulloch

Published by New Generation Publishing in 2020

First Edition

ISBN 978-1-80031-983-7

www.newgeneration-publishing.com

 New Generation Publishing

Thank you to all production staff for their help and advice.

Thanks to the staff at Edinburgh City Libraries who granted permission for use of the front cover image.

Dedication

To my two grandchildren, Lewis and Abi
and also my wife Joyce.

With thanks to Ann Meikle for her help
with the manuscript.

Foreword

I am delighted to write this foreword, not only because Robert McCulloch is a friend but because of our shared love of Edinburgh. Bob has done a great deal for the City including, for example, initiating and operating certificates and qualifications in tourism for taxi drivers. 'A Good Night Out' is a reflection of modern Edinburgh but also a knowledgeable look back at life in the Capital in the not too distant past. It gives us an insight into how people lived in this great city and explores the thoughts and habits of Scottish society now largely gone. We find ourselves in that magical space where things are half remembered but seem so different from today. Bob's immense knowledge and storytelling abilities make 'A Good Night Out' a compelling read. People and places are brought back to life. Bob's love of the history of Edinburgh is well-known, but to put it in writing makes it available for generations to come. People who think they know a lot about the city will be fascinated to discover the facts behind the stories and the way things came about. The reach of 'A Good Night Out' goes well beyond the boundaries of the city, tracing back the development of the film industry and how it affected people's thinking, such as in 'Gene Autry's Cowboy Code' all the way to 'Buck Rogers'. From theatre to football; song and dance, it's all here. If you are interested in Edinburgh and history, you will not be able to put this book down. Bob's life as a 'cabbie' and guide in Edinburgh has given him a unique and in-depth insight into the city's people and buildings.

Donald Wilson has been a Councillor representing the Sighthill/Gorgie ward since 1999, holding various positions in the City including Vice-Convenor of the Economic Development Committee and Executive Member for Modernising Government. He has chaired the Edinburgh International Science Festival, Edinburgh and

Lothians Tourist Board and the Edinburgh Convention Bureau. As past Lord Provost he was Chair of a number of organisations including the Edinburgh International Festival and the Royal Edinburgh Military Tattoo. At this time he was also the Lord Lieutenant which is the Queen's representative in the City. He is presently Convener of the Culture and Communities Committee and Deacon of the Incorporation of Baxters of the City of Edinburgh.

CONTENTS

Introduction

Edinburgh today is a vibrant city and a must visit place for the many tourists who come to attend the numerous festivals held annually, and is rightly known as The Festival City.

From the historical "Old Town" to the grandeur and elegance of the Georgian "New Town".

The city has been home, either through birth or choice to many famous and influential people who have made a vast contribution to the world as we know it today.

It no longer boasts large printing companies, brewing companies engineering works or shipbuilders yards but instead has become the home of financial institutions and the banking sector making it one of the main financial centres in the world.

Many of the things today we take for granted are recent developments but in the not too distant past things were very different.

The citizens of Edinburgh once had a wide variety of ways to spend their recreational time. Although most now are just a fading memory, there was everything from roller skating to ice skating, wrestling to dancing,(although sometimes it seemed to be the same) speedway to pony trotting, stock car racing to saloon car racing, skiing, curling, greyhound racing and professional sprinting.

Cinemas

Chapter 1

There was also an abundance of cinemas and strange as it may seem today the front page of the Evening News carried a list of the cinemas and their programmes. Before the advent of television most cinemas changed their programme twice a week, Monday to Wednesday, Thursday to Saturday. With two films, a cartoon, a Pathe News bulletin, an advertising feature from Pearl and Dean and trailers for forthcoming attractions in a show that would last for three and a half hours. When the show finished God Save The Queen was played and all the audience would stand. It was good value for money. The fact that most districts had their own local picture house meant that most people went once a week and the children had their own Saturday morning or afternoon shows.

The first picture shows were staged in tents by showmen at fairgrounds and many cinema owning families started this way. One of them was "Captain Texas" who brought the fairground spirit to the Imperial picture house in Leith where he would regularly shoot a clay pipe or cigarette out of the mouth of his daughter.

The Cinematographic Act of 1909 effectively took film shows out of the fairgrounds and into cinemas. The Act required that projection booths be separate from the main auditorium as a fire precaution and toilet facilities had to be provided so that effectively marked the end of tents as venues.

A new group of people were now entering the scene such as F.R. Graham-Yool, a scrap metal dealer, J. Maguire a bookie and his partner racetrack owner F. Lumley and JKS Poole whose family came from a fairground background.

They would go on to be the driving force in the new form of entertainment, building some of the best theatres in town. A survey shows that in the 1940's there was a seat for every fifteen people in the city with most going once or twice a week.

The difference in auditoriums varied greatly. The Playhouse which was the largest seated three thousand and was the second biggest in Scotland, down to a local one seating only one hundred. The optimum size for making a profit was found to be 1,500 and so all new theatres would seat that number. The Palace on Princes Street was built in 1913 at a cost of £10,000.

Many were built in the Art Deco style and two of the best architects were T. Bowhill Gibson and W.R. Lambe. Probably the best known of T. Bowhill Gibson's work was the County (later the George) in Bath Street, Portobello. It was the last picture house to be built in the city and it opened in 1939 showing *Snow White and the Seven Dwarfs*. It closed as a cinema in 1974 and is now (surprisingly) a bingo hall.

In the poorer areas the local cinema was often nicknamed "The Gaff" or "The Fleapit", usually accurately (you itch to get in and scratch when you come out). In Brendon Thomas's "The Last Picture Show" he states that in the "Starry" in St. Mary's Street, boy patrons were not expected to leave their seats to relieve themselves but did so against the back of the seat in front, being rewarded with a squirt of disinfectant from a syringe wielded by an usherette. In the New Palace in the High Street, opposite John Knox's house the patrons in the balcony pelted the patrons in the stalls with shells from "Buckies" (a type of shell fish) that they had purchased from a fish wife who had a stall outside the front door. When the cinema closed in September 1956 it was reported in the Evening News that when the youthful audience tried singing "Auld Lang Syne" the usherette shouted "Stop the racket! You're barred the lot of you, you will not get in next week".

Rumour had it she married the manager, not so surprising as she carried a torch for him for years.

Some theatres had unique features such as the Poole's Synod Hall on Castle Terrace which specialized in horror films so patrons had to be sixteen to gain admission, not that anyone was ever refused entry. This was a bit at odds with its former use as the Synod Halls of the United Presbyterian Church. The auditorium was horseshoe shaped with the seats on the side at right angles to the screen so that by the time the show ended you had a crick in your neck. The New Tivoli on Gorgie Road had double seats, without centre arm rests known as "chummy seats" in the back row, always a favourite with courting couples. There was mood lighting controlled by the projectionist, and for "Dracula" films it was always dark blue. The "Tiv" as it was known closed as a cinema in 1973 and was used as a bingo hall until the smoking ban led to its closure. It is now a religious centre for the Destiny church.

Many of the theatres were family owned; the last one being the Dominion on Newbattle Terrace, the patrons would all know the proprietor often by his first name. Others belonged to a national chain and some were tied to a particular Hollywood studio, for example the Roxy on Gorgie Road had an arrangement with Twentieth Century Fox and the New Tivoli had the same with Metro Goldwyn Mayer, (MGM). The man best known in the industry was J.K.S. Poole whose family were traveling show people. They came to town in 1906 and decided to settle down opening several cinemas. The Poole's Roxy was well known for the Mickey Mouse Club on a Saturday morning but the club started in the Tivoli also on Gorgie Road where it ran from 1934 to 1938. Children's clubs operated in most cinemas on a Saturday morning or afternoon and some kids who had generous parents could go to each performance in different cinemas. The films on offer were always action adventure dominated by westerns or cowboy films as they were known. Some of the stars were Roy Rogers with his wife Dale Evans, with their horses Trigger and Buttermilk and Alsatian dog Bullet. Actor Bill Boyd who was Hopalong Cassidy (Hoppy) with his horse Topper. They all three visited the city in the 1950's for publicity purposes. A photo shoot was arranged in which Roy Rogers was seen leading Trigger down the staircase of the Caledonian Hotel leading children to believe the horse was staying in the hotel when in fact he was stabled in the Co-Operative stables on Grove Street.

Other favourites were Gene Autry "the singing cowboy" and his horse Champion, the Lone Ranger (actor Clayton Moore) his horse Silver (HI Ho Silver) and Tonto played by actor Jay Siverheels his Indian companion, who always addressed him as "Kemosabe" meaning faithful friend in the Indian dialect and his horse Scout. Tom Mix and his horse Tony, Zorro "the flashing blade", Superman, Batman and Robin all were heroes to kids in the 40's and 50's and with the programmes of a serial cliff hanger type there was always a queue the following week to see if the hero survived. It was not unknown for small boys to smuggle (you were searched at the door) pistols and holsters into the auditorium, and some kids had the full Lone Ranger outfit with hat, mask, six gun and holster so they could shoot the "baddies" and help their hero with a shout of "he's behind you!". Sometimes the audience became so noisy that the film was stopped and the lights went on so that the usherettes could restore order. It was not only small boys who caused problems for the management. When *Jailhouse Rock* starring Elvis Presley was screened in the Lyceum on Slateford Road so many teenagers started jiving in the aisles that everyone was ejected, only to form a queue and pay for admission again. In what, nowadays might seem a strange way of running a cinema, the management decided to refuse admission to anybody wearing jeans. With television becoming more popular many cinemas had to close or change their programmes. Some specialized in horror films or soft porn and it is interesting to note that those showing X certificate films went out of business while the Dominion which never showed an X rated film until the mid 70's and catered to the family audience is still going strong. It can boast to be the only cinema with a restaurant and gift shop run by the management. Some went continental or art house, some to multi screen while most seemed to opt for the dreaded bingo or only slightly better demolition. The golden age of Hollywood coincided with the peak viewing figures of British cinemas in the 1940's-50's when it was not unusual to queue for an hour to gain admission to see their favourite star. Anyone with a sense of nostalgia can see these films on television on what seems like a daily basis.

Chapter 2

The Big Six Hollywood Studios were controlled by a group of ruthless businessmen who kept their stars under close scrutiny, nothing was allowed to tarnish the image they presented to the world with their publicity departments covering up sexual indiscretions, drug abuse and alcoholism.

Once the largest, most glamorous, and most revered film studio, MGM was founded in 1924 when the entertainment entrepreneur Marcus Leowe gained control of Metro Pictures, Goldwyn Pictures, and Louis B Mayer Pictures. Its headquarters are in Beverley Hills California. It is one of the world's oldest film studios.

MGM's biggest cartoon stars would come in the form of the cat-and-mouse duo Tom and Jerry created by William Hanna and Joseph Barbera in 1940. The *Tom and Jerry* cartoons won seven Academy Awards between 1943 and 1953. In 1941, the legendary animator Tex Avery left a successful career at Warner Bros and joined the company giving it status. He left in 1953.

The studio's official motto, "*Ars Gratia Artis*", is a Latin phrase meaning "Art For Arts Sake". It was chosen by Howard Dietz the studio's chief publicist. The studio's logo is a roaring lion surrounded by a ring of film inscribed with the studio's motto. The logo, which features Leo the Lion by Dietz in 1916 for Goldwyn Pictures and updated in 1924 for MGM's use. Dietz based the logo on his alma mater's mascot, the Columbia University lion. Originally silent, the sound of Leo the Lion's roar was added to films for the first time in August 1928. In the 1930s and 1940s, the studio billed itself as having "more stars than there are in heaven", a reference to the large number of A list movie stars under contract to the company. This second motto was also coined by Dietz and was first used in 1932.

Paramount Pictures Corporation (also known simply as Paramount) is an American film studio based in Hollywood California, that has been a subsidiary of the American media-conglomerate Viacom since 1994. Paramount is the fifth oldest surviving film studio in the world, the second oldest in the United States, and the sole member of the "Big Six" film studios still located in the Los Angeles neighbourhood of Hollywood. In 1916, film producer Alfred Zuckor contracted 22 actors and actresses and honoured each with a star on the logo. These fortunate few would become the first "movie stars." These included Douglas Fairbanks, Gloria Swanston and Rudolph Valentino. In 2014, Paramount Pictures became the first major Hollywood studio to distribute all of its films in digital form only.

Twentieth Century pictures owners Joseph Shenck and Daryll F Zanuck who left United Artists over a stock dispute began merger talks with struggling Fox films. After the merger the studios biggest star Will Rogers died in a plane crash and promising young actor Spencer Tracy was suspended because of his heavy drinking.

Zanuck quickly signed young actors who would carry Twentieth Century-Fox for years: Tyrone Power, Linda Darnell, Carmen Miranda, Don Ameche Henry Fonda, Gene Teirney, Sonia Henjie, and Betty Grable Also on the Fox payroll he found two players who he built up into the studio's leading assets, Alice Faye and seven-year-old Shirley Temple. Favouring popular biographies and musicals, Zanuck built Fox back to profitability. Thanks to record attendance during World War II, Fox overtook RKO and Metro-Goldwyn-Mayer (Hollywood's biggest studio) to become the third most profitable film studio. While Zanuck went off for eighteen months' war service, junior partner William Goetz kept profits high by going for light entertainment. The studio's—indeed the industry's—biggest star was creamy blonde Betty Grable.

Fox also produced film versions of Broadway musicals, including in 1945 the Rogers and Hammerstein films, beginning with the musical version of *State Fair*, the only work that the famous team wrote especially for films and continuing years later with *Carousel, The King and I* and *The Sound of Music.* They also made the 1958 film version of *South Pacific*.

Many of the Hollywood musicals were dubbed by ghost singers who never received credit for their work. The secret world of the 'ghost singers' who provided the vocals for the screen legends who did not sing their own songs in the great Hollywood musicals was only brought to light recently.

Marni Nixon, Betty Noyes and Bill Lee aren't household names... but they should be. During a prolific era of "ghost-voicing" in Hollywood musicals, they sang as, respectively, Audrey Hepburn, Debbie Reynolds and Christopher Plummer. As far as the movie moguls were concerned, it was a trade secret and should remain one. This meant that, for years, cinema goers thought that Natalie Wood was actually singing as Maria in *West Side Story,* and Mark Lester in the lead role of *Oliver!* The former was famously disgruntled at her version of I Feel Pretty being sung over. Lester, on the other hand, was thrilled at his perfect pitch (courtesy of Kathe Green, daughter of the film's musical director). As Lester now says, "You wouldn't want me to sing. It would destroy that wonderful image of that little boy singing. Just don't go there!". Betty Noyes is also known for singing the song "Baby Mine" in the Disney film *Dumbo* (1941), which was nominated for the Academy Award for Best Original Song. However she was not given screen credit for this performance (no voice actors were for *Dumbo*).

United Artists (UA) is an American film and television entertainment studio founded in 1919 by D.W.Griffiths, Charlie Chaplin, Mary Pickford and Douglas Fairbanks who were disgruntled by the studios treatment of them and their lack of artistic input The studios were premised on allowing actors to control their own interests, rather than being dependent upon commercial studios. UA was repeatedly bought, sold and restructured over the ensuing century. The current United Artists company is a successor to the original in name only: the studio was acquired by Metro-Goldwyn-Mayer in 1981.

The brothers Harry, Albert, Sam and Jack Warner were Polish immigrants who started off in theatre management before moving into the film industry. With the studio struggling its biggest star was a dog -Rin-Tin-Tin who Jack referred to as the mortgage lifter paying the dogs owner, a former soldier $1000 per picture.

With the collapse of the market for musicals, Warner Bros., under Zanuck turned to more socially realistic story lines. For its many films about gangsters; Warner Bros. soon became known as a "gangster studio". The studio's first gangster film, *Little Caesar*, was a great box office success and the star, Edward G. Robinson would go on to reprise the character in many of the subsequent Warner gangster films. The studio's next effort, *The Public Enemy*, made James Cagney arguably the studio's new top star. Also under contract were Humphrey Bogart and George Raft and in a lighter vein Warner Bros. made a series of cartoons under the name Merrie Melodies with Bugs Bunny, Daffy Duck, Tweety Pie and Sylvester and Porky Pig whose stutter was due to the voice actor who had a speech impediment. To keep production time down it was decided to leave in the stutter. This led to Porky stumbling over simple words and replacing them with longer more difficult ones. At the end of a film Porky would burst through a bass drum and say "Th Th The Th Th "Thats All Folks" instead of "The End". When Mel Blanc took over voicing Porky he kept in the stutter.

Chapter 3

Mel Blanc (May 30, 1908 – July 10, 1989) was a voice actor, actor, radio comedian, and recording artist. He began his 60-plus-year career performing in radio, but is best remembered for his work in animation as the voices of Bugs Bunny, Daffy Duck, Porky Pig, Tweety Pie, Sylvester the Cat, Yosemite Sam, Foghorn Leghorn, Marvin the Martian, Pepé Le Pew, Speedy Gonzales, Wile E. Coyote, Road Runner, the Tasmanian Devil, and many of the other characters from the *Looney Tunes* and *Merrie Melodies* theatrical cartoons during the golden age of American animation. He was, in fact, the voice for all of the major male Warner Bros. cartoon characters except for Elmer Fudd, whose voice was provided (uncredited) by fellow radio actor Arthur Q. Bryan, although Blanc later voiced Fudd as well after Bryan's death. He later worked for Hanna-Barbera's television cartoons, most notably as the voices of Barney Rubble on *The Flintstones* and Mr. Spacely on *The Jetsons*. Blanc was also the original voice of Universal Pictures, and provided vocal effects for the *Tom and Jerry* cartoons directed by Chuck Jones and Woody Woodpecker. Furthermore, during the golden age of radio, Blanc was a frequent performer on the radio programs of famous comedians from the era, including Jack Benny, Abbott and Costello, Burns and Allen. Having earned the nickname "The Man of a Thousand Voices", Blanc is regarded as one of the most influential people in the voice-acting industry. The inscription on his tombstone reads "thats all folks".

The accolade of best animator must go to Walter Elias Disney(Dec 5, 1901- Dec 15, 1966). He was an American entrepreneur, animator, voice actor and film producer. A pioneer of the American animation industry, he introduced several developments in the production of cartoons. As a film producer, Disney holds the record for most Academy

Awards earned by an individual, having won 22 Oscars from 59 nominations. He was presented with two Golden Globe Special Achievement Awards and an Emmy Award, among other honours. Several of his films are included in the National Film Registry by the Library of Congress.

Born in Chicago in 1901, Disney developed an early interest in drawing. He took art classes as a boy and got a job as a commercial illustrator at the age of 18. He moved to California in the early 1920s and set up the Disney Brothers Studio with his brother Roy, Walt developed the character Mickey Mouse in 1928, his first highly popular success; he also provided the voice for his creation in the early years. As the studio grew, Disney became more adventurous, introducing synchronized sound, full-color three-strip Technicolor, feature-length cartoons and technical developments in cameras. The results, seen in features such as *Snow White and the Seven Dwarfs* (1937), *Fantasia*, *Pinocchio* (both 1940), *Dumbo* (1941) and *Bambi* (1942), furthered the development of animated film. New animated and live-action films followed after World War II, including the critically successful *Cinderella* (1950) and *Mary Poppins* (1964), the latter of which received five Academy Awards.

In the 1950s, Disney expanded into the amusement park industry, and in 1955 he opened Disneyland. To fund the project he diversified into television programs, such as *Walt Disney's Disneyland* and *The Mickey Mouse Club*; he was also involved in planning the 1959 Moscow Fair, the 1960 Winter Olympics, and the 1964 New York World's Fair. In 1965, he began development of another theme park, Disney World, the heart of which was to be a new type of city, the "Experimental Prototype Community of Tomorrow" (EPCOT). Disney was a heavy smoker throughout his life, and died of lung cancer in December 1966 before either the park or the EPCOT project were completed.

In the silent era of Hollywood, slapstick ruled and the greatest proponent of this genre was,

"Charlie" Chaplin, (16 April 1889 – 25 Dec. 1977) who was an English comic actor, film-maker, and composer who rose to fame in the era of silent film. Chaplin became a worldwide icon through his screen persona "the Tramp" and is considered one of the most important figures in the history of the film industry. His career spanned more than 75 years, from childhood in the Victorian era until a year before his death in 1977, and encompassed both adulation and controversy. Chaplin's childhood in London was one of poverty and hardship. As his father was absent and his mother struggled financially, he was sent to a workhouse twice before the age of nine. When he was 14, his mother was committed to a mental asylum. Chaplin began performing at an early age, touring music halls and later working as a stage actor and comedian. At 19, he was signed to the prestigious Fred Karno company, which took him to America. Chaplin was scouted for the film industry and began appearing in 1914 for Keystone Studios. He soon developed the Tramp persona and formed a large fan base. Chaplin directed his own films from an early stage and continued to hone his craft as he moved to the Essanay, Mutual, and First National corporations. By 1918, he was one of the best-known figures in the world. In 1919, Chaplin co-founded the distribution company United Artists, which gave him complete control over his films. His first feature-length was *The Kid* (1921), followed by *A Woman of Paris* (1923), *The Gold Rush* (1925), and *The Circus* (1928). He refused to move to sound films in the 1930s, instead producing *City Lights* (1931) and *Modern Times* (1936) without dialogue. Chaplin became increasingly political, and his next film, *The Great Dictator* (1940), satirized Adolf Hitler. The 1940s were a decade marked with controversy for Chaplin, and his popularity declined rapidly. He was accused of communist sympathies, while his involvement in a paternity suit and marriages to much younger women caused scandal. An FBI investigation was opened, and Chaplin was forced to leave the United States and settle in Switzerland. Years later it was revealed that the allegations were spurious and he could return at any time, but he never did. He abandoned the Tramp in his later films, which include *Monsieur Verdoux* (1947), *Limelight* (1952), *A King in New York* (1957), and *A Countess from Hong Kong* (1967).Chaplin wrote, directed, produced, edited, starred in, and composed the music for most of his films. He was a perfectionist, and his financial independence enabled him to spend years on the development and production of a picture. His films are characterized by slapstick combined with pathos, typified in the Tramp's struggles against adversity. Many contain social and political themes, as well as autobiographical elements. In 1972, as part of a renewed appreciation for his work, Chaplin received an Academy Award for "the incalculable effect he has had in making motion pictures the art form of this century". He continues to be held in high regard, with *The Gold Rush*, *City Lights*, *Modern Times*, and *The Great Dictator* often ranked on industry lists of the greatest films of all time.

Alongside Chaplin was "Buster" Keaton (Oct.4, 1895 – Feb. 1, 1966) an American actor, comedian, film director, producer, screenwriter, and stunt performer. He was best known for his silent films, in which his trademark was physical comedy with a consistently stoic, deadpan expression, earning him the nickname "The Great Stone Face". Critic Roger Ebert wrote of Keaton's extraordinary period from 1920 to 1929, when he worked without interruption on a series of films that make him, arguably, the greatest actor–director in the history of the movies. His career declined afterwards with a dispiriting loss of his artistic independence when he was hired by Metro-Goldwyn-Mayer and he descended into alcoholism, ruining his family life. He recovered in the 1940s, remarried, and revived his career to a degree as an honoured comic performer for the rest of his life, earning an Academy Honorary Award in 1959.Many of Keaton's films from the 1920s, such as *Sherlock Jr.* (1924), *The General* (1926), and *The Cameraman* (1928), remain highly regarded, with the second of these three widely viewed as his masterpiece. Among its strongest admirers was Orson Welles, who stated that *The General* was cinema's highest achievement in comedy, and perhaps the greatest film ever made. Keaton was recognized as the seventh-greatest film director by *Entertainment Weekly*, and in 1999, the American Film Institute ranked him the 21st greatest male star of classic Hollywood cinema.

The silent era also gave us the antics of The Keystone Cops (often spelled "Keystone Kops") who were fictional incompetent policemen, featured in silent film comedies in the early 20th century. The movies were produced by Mack Sennett for his Keystone Film Company between 1912 and 1917. Each film had a different cast. The name has since been used to criticize any group for its mistakes, particularly if the mistakes happened after a great deal of energy and activity, or for a lack of coordination among the members.

Chapter 4

Westerns or cowboy films as they were known were the staple diet of post war film makers and the stars became heroes to thousands of young boys. One of the earliest was Tom Mix; (Jan 6, 1880 – Oct12, 1940) the star of many early Western movies between 1909 and 1935. Mix appeared in 291 films, all but nine of which were silent movies. He was Hollywood's first Western star and helped define the genre as it emerged in the early days of the cinema. Heroes and villains were sharply defined with the goodie wearing a white hat and the baddie wearing a black hat and a clean-cut cowboy always saved the day. Millions of children grew up watching his films on Saturday afternoons. His intelligent and handsome horse Tony also became a celebrity. Mix did his own stunts and was frequently injured. In 1929, Mix was a pallbearer at the funeral of Wyatt Earp.

Whilst driving to Phoenix Arizona Mix came upon construction barriers at a bridge washed away by a flash flood. Unable to stop in time, his car swerved twice, then overturned in a gully. A large aluminum suitcase containing money, traveler's cheques, and jewels, situated on the package shelf behind his head, hurled forward and struck him, killing him by breaking his neck. He was 60 years old.

Mix was the acknowledged "King of Cowboys" when Ronald Reagan and John Wayne were young, and the influence of his screen persona can be seen in their approach to portraying cowboys. When an injury caused football player Marion Morrison (later known as John Wayne) to drop out of the University of Southern California, Mix helped him find work moving props in the back lot of Fox Studios. That was the beginning of Wayne's Hollywood career.

One character who successfully made the transition from silver screen to television screen was Hopalong Cassidy or "Hop-along" Cassidy. He was a fictional cowboy hero created in 1904 by the author Clarence E. Mulford, who wrote a series of popular short stories and many novels based on the character.

In his early writings, Mulford portrayed the character as rude, dangerous, and rough-talking. He had a wooden leg which caused him to walk with a little "hop", hence the nickname. From 1935, the character was played by movie actor William Boyd in films adapted from Mulford's books and was transformed into a clean-cut, sarsaparilla-drinking hero. Sixty-six popular films appeared, only a few of which were loosely based on Mulford's stories.

As portrayed on the screen, white-haired Bill "Hopalong" Cassidy was usually clad strikingly in black (including his hat, an exception to the western film stereotype that only villains wore black hats). He was reserved and well spoken, with a sense of fair play. He was often called upon to intercede when dishonest characters took advantage of honest citizens. "Hoppy" and his white horse, Topper, usually traveled through the west with two companions—one young and trouble-prone with a weakness for damsels in distress, the other older, comically awkward and outspoken. After 66 films studios stopped production in 1944. Boyd resumed production in 1946, on lower budgets, and continued through 1948, when "B" westerns were being phased out. Boyd thought Hopalong Cassidy might have a future in television, spending $350,000 to obtain the rights to his old films, and approached the fledgling NBC network. The initial broadcasts were so successful that NBC could not wait for a television series to be produced and edited the feature films to broadcast length. On June 24, 1949, *Hopalong Cassidy* became the first network Western television series. The success of the television series made Boyd a star. In January 1950 The Mutual Broadcasting System began broadcasting a radio version, with Andy Clyde as the sidekick, and at the end of September, the show moved to CBS Radio, where it ran until 1952.The series and character were so popular that Hopalong Cassidy was featured on the cover of national magazines such as *Look, Life*, and *Time*. Boyd earned millions as Hopalong ($800,000 in 1950 alone), mostly from merchandise licensing and endorsement deals. In 1950, Hopalong Cassidy was featured on the first lunchbox to bear an image, causing sales for Aladdin Industries to jump from 50,000 to 600,000 in one year. More than 100 companies in 1950 manufactured $70 million of Hopalong Cassidy products, including children's dinnerware, pillows, roller skates, soap, wristwatches, and jackknives.

Gabby Hayes was probably the most famous sidekick in Western movies during the 1930's and 1940's, playing opposite Randolph Scott, Roy Rogers, Wild Bill Elliott and, of course, Hopalong Cassidy in more than 40 cowboy films.

With the coming of sound it seemed a good idea to have a "singing cowboy" and many films were made where the central character would burst into song. The first of these was Gene Autry (Sept 29, 1907 – Oct 2, 1998) an American performer who gained fame as a singing cowboy on the radio, in movies, and on television for more than three decades beginning in the early 1930s. Autry was also owner of a television station, several radio stations in Southern California, and the Los Angeles/ California/Anaheim Angels Major League Baseball team from 1961 to 1997.

From 1934 to 1953, Autry appeared in 93 films and 91 episodes of *The Gene Autry Show* television series. During the 1930s and 1940s, he personified the straight-shooting hero—honest, brave, and true—and profoundly touched the lives of millions of Americans. Autry was also one of the most important figures in the history of country music, considered the second major influential artist of the genre's development after Jimmie Rodgers. His singing cowboy movies were the first vehicle to carry country music to a national audience. In addition to his signature song, "Back in the Saddle Again", Autry is still remembered for his Christmas holiday songs, "Here Comes Santa Claus", which he wrote, "Frosty the Snowman", "An Old Fashioned Tree", and his biggest hit, "Rudolph the Red-Nosed Reindeer".

Autry was a member of both the Country Music Hall of Fame and Nashville Songwriters Hall of Fame, and is the only person to be awarded stars in all five categories on the Hollywood Walk of Fame, for film, television, music, radio, and live performance. The town of Gene Autry, Oklahoma was named in his honour.

In response to his many young radio listeners aspiring to emulate him, Autry created the Cowboy Code,

He must not hit a smaller man,

He must not take unfair advantage.

He must never go back on his word, or a trust confided in him.

He must always tell the truth.

He must be gentle with children, the elderly, and animals.

He must not advocate or possess racially or religiously intolerant ideas.

He must help people in distress.

He must be a good worker.

He must keep himself clean in thought, speech, action, and personal habits.

He must respect women, parents, and his nation's laws.

The Cowboy is a patriot.

Autry retired from show business in 1964, having made almost 100 films up to 1955 and over 600 records.

Next to appear was Roy Rogers (born Leonard Franklin Slye, November 5, 1911 – July 6, 1998) the singer and actor who was one of the most popular Western stars of his era. Known as the "King of the Cowboys", he appeared in over 100 films and numerous radio and television episodes of *The Roy Rogers Show*. In many of his films and television episodes, he appeared with his wife, Dale

Evans; his golden palomino, Trigger; and his German shepherd dog, Bullet. His show was broadcast on radio for nine years and then on television from 1951 through 1957. His productions usually featured a sidekick, often Pat Brady, Andy Devine, George "Gabby" Hayes, or Smiley Burnette. On a publicity tour whilst staying in the Caledonian Hotel. Chief Constable of the Lothian & Peebles Constabulary "Wee" Willie Merrilees OBE took him on a visit to Dunforth Lodge orphanage. While there a young girl named Marion Fleming sang a song "Will you buy my pretty flowers". Dale Evans was so moved that she asked if they could take her home to live on their ranch. "Wee" Willie arranged for it to happen.

So popular was Rogers that he lent his name to over 400 merchandising items, second only to Walt Disney. It was stated by his manager that over $1 billion dollars was spent on products carrying his name.

The weekly Roy Rogers comic sold in excess of !.3 million copies a week and the Roy Rogers annual was a must have for many small boys at Christmas.

The portrayal of the leading man in westerns as the strong silent type was personified by Randolph Scott (Jan 23, 1898 – March 2, 1987) a film actor whose career spanned from 1928 to 1962. As a leading man for all but the first three years of his cinematic career, Scott appeared in a variety of genres, including social dramas, crime dramas, comedies, musicals (albeit in non-singing and non-dancing roles), adventure tales, war films, and a few horror and fantasy films. However, his most enduring image is that of the tall-in-the-saddle Western hero. Out of his more than 100 film appearances over 60 were in Westerns; thus, of all the major stars whose names were associated with the Western, Scott most closely identified with it.

Tall (6ft 2½ in), lanky and handsome, Scott displayed an easygoing charm and courtly Southern drawl in his early films that helped offset his limitations as an actor, where he was frequently found to be stiff or lumbering. As he matured, however, Scott's acting improved while his features became burnished and leathery, turning him into the ideal "strong, silent" type of hero.

The Western films portrayed the hero as a man of high values and an unshakeable belief that they would win through and this was typical of the films of one man, John Wayne (born Marion Robert Morrison; May 26, 1907 – June 11, 1979), nicknamed Duke, was an American actor and film-maker. An Academy Award-winner for *True Grit* (1969), Wayne was among the top box office draws for three decades.

As a favour to USC football coach Howard Jones, who had given silent western film star Tom Mix tickets to USC games, director John Ford and Mix hired Wayne as a prop boy and extra. Wayne later credited his walk, talk, and persona to his acquaintance with Wyatt Earp, who was good friends with Tom Mix

For his screen name, director Raol Walsh suggested "Anthony Wayne", after Revolutionary War General "Mad Anthony Wayne", but Fox Studios chief Winfield Sheehan rejected it as sounding "too Italian". Walsh then suggested "John Wayne". Sheehan agreed, and the name was set. Wayne was not even present for the discussion.

He was president of Glendale High class of 1925. He found work at local film studios when he lost his football scholarship to the University of Southern California as a result of a bodysurfing accident. Initially working for the Fox Film Corporation, he appeared mostly in small bit parts. His first leading role came in Raoul Walsh's *The Big Trail* (1930), which led to leading roles in numerous B movies throughout the 1930s, many of them in the Western genre.

Wayne's career took off in 1939, with John Ford's *Stagecoach* making him an instant star. He went on to star in 142 pictures. Biographer Ronald Davis said, "John Wayne personified for millions the nation's frontier heritage. Eighty-three of his movies were Westerns, and in them he played cowboys, cavalrymen, and unconquerable loners extracted from the Republic's central creation myth."

Wayne's other well-known Western roles include a cattleman driving his herd north on the Chisholm Trail in *Red River* (1948), a Civil War veteran whose young niece is abducted by a tribe of Commance Indians in *The Searchers* (1956), and a troubled rancher competing with a lawyer for a woman's hand in marriage in *The Man Who Shot Liberty Valance* (1962). He is also remembered for his roles in *The Quiet Man* (1952), *Rio Bravo* (1959), and *The Longest Day* (1962). In his final screen performance, he starred as an ageing gunfighter battling cancer in *The Shootist* (1976). He appeared with many important Hollywood stars of his era, and his last public appearance was at the Academy Awards ceremony on April 9, 1979.

The influence that Waynes films had on the audience was immence. One line of dialogue" that'll be the day" from his hit film *The Searchers* inspired Buddy Holly to write a song of the same name.

Making the successful transition from silver screen to television screen was The Lone Ranger a masked former Texas Ranger who fought outlaws in the American Old West with his Native American friend, Tonto. The character has been called an enduring icon of American culture The title character was played on the radio show by George Seaton, Earle Graser, and Brace Beemer. Clayton Moore portrayed the Lone Ranger on television, although during a contract dispute, Moore was replaced temporarily by John Hart, who wore a different style of mask. On the radio, Tonto was played by, among others, John Todd and Roland Parker; and in the television series, by Jay Silverheels, who was a Mohawk from the Six Nations Indian Reserve in Ontario, Canada. Tonto always referred to the Lone Ranger as Kemosabe. which means faithful friend. The Lone Ranger's horse was called Silver and Tonto's was Scout. The theme music to *The Lone Ranger* is March of the Swiss Soldiers, the finale of Rossini's *William Tell Overture*.

Another masked hero was Zorro (Spanish for "fox") it was the secret identity of Don Diego de la Vega, a fictional character created in 1919 by pulp writer Johnston McCulley. He was a Californio living in Los Angeles during the era of Mexican California (between 1821 and 1846), although some movie adaptations of Zorro's story have placed him during the earlier Spanish Rule. The character has undergone changes through the years, but the typical image of him is a dashing black-clad masked outlaw who defends the commoners and indigenous peoples of the land against tyrannical officials and other villains. Not only is he too cunning and fox like for the bumbling authorities to catch, but he also delights in publicly humiliating them His favoured weapon is a rapier, which he often uses to leave his distinctive mark, a *Z* cut with three quick strokes. He also uses a bullwhip.

Clarence Linden Crabbe II February 7, 1908 – April 23, 1983), commonly known by his stage name Buster Crabbe, was an American two-time Olympic swimmer and movie actor. He won the 1932 Olympic gold medal for 400-metre freestyle swimming event before breaking into acting.

He held 15 world records and 35 national records. He starred in a number of popular films in the 1930s and 1940s. He also played the title role in the serials *Tarzan the Fearless*, *Flash Gordon* and *Buck Rogers.* Crabbe is the only actor to play Tarzan, Flash Gordon and Buck Rogers – the top three syndicated comic strip heroes of the 1930s.

A 12-part Buck Rogers serial film was produced in 1939 by Universal Pictures Company. Buck Rogers (Buster Crabbe) and his young friend Buddy Wade get caught in a blizzard and are forced to crash their airship in the Arctic wastes. In order to survive until they can be rescued, they inhale their supply of Nirvano gas which puts them in a state of suspended animation. When they are eventually rescued by scientists, they learn that 500 years have passed. It is now 2440. A tyrannical dictator named Killer Kane and his henchmen now run the world. Buck and Buddy must now save the world, and they do so with the help of Lieutenant Wilma Deering and Prince Tallen of Saturn.

The serial had a small budget and saved money on special effects by reusing material from other stories: background shots from the futuristic musical *Just Imagine* (1930), as the city of the future, the garishly stenciled walls from the Azura palace set in *Flash Gordon's Trip to Mars*, as Kane's penthouse suite, and even the studded leather belt that Crabbe wore in *Flash Gordon's Trip to Mars* turned up as part of Buck's uniform. Between 1953 and the mid-1970s, this film serial was edited into three distinct feature film versions.

Moving into the realm of the superhero gave us Superman who was born on an alien world to a technologically advanced species that resembles humans. When his world is on the verge of destruction, his father, a scientist, places his infant son alone in a spaceship that takes him to Earth. The earliest newspaper strips name the planet "Krypton", the baby "Kal-L", and his biological parents "Jor-L" and "Lora" their names become "Jor-el", and "Lara" in a 1942 spin-off novel by George Lowther. The ship lands in the American countryside, where the baby is adopted by the Kents. In the original stories, they adopt him from an orphanage. The Kents name the boy Clark and raise him in a farming community.

The Kents teach Clark he must conceal his otherworldly origins and use his fantastic powers to do good. Clark creates the costumed identity of Superman so as to protect his personal privacy and the safety of his loved ones. As Clark Kent, he wears eyeglasses to disguise his face and wears his Superman costume underneath his clothes so that he can change at a moment's notice. To complete this disguise, Clark avoids violent confrontation, preferring to slip away and change into Superman often in a phone booth when danger arises, and suffers occasional ridicule for his apparent cowardice.

Chapter 5

Comedy films were always a safe bet for the studios with some being churned out on a weekly basis one of the most enduring partnerships was Laurel and Hardy who were a comedy double act during the early Classical Hollywood era of American cinema. The team was composed of English thin man Stan Laurel (1890–1965) and American fat man Oliver Hardy (1892–1957). They became well known during the late 1920s through the mid-1940s for their slapstick comedy, with Laurel playing the clumsy and childlike friend of the pompous bully Hardy. The catchphrase "thats another fine mess you've got me into" was used in most of their films. The duo's signature tune is known variously as "The Cuckoo Song", "Ku-Ku", or "The Dance of the Cuckoos". It was played over the opening credits of their films and has become as emblematic of the duo as their bowler hats. They appeared as a team in 107 films, starring in 32 short silent films, 40 short sound films, and 23 full-length feature films.

When Hardy died Laurel stopped making films despite numerous financially good offers. He spent the rest of his life answering fan mail and meeting fans.

Always very popular were the Marx Brothers who were an American family comedy act that was successful in vaudeville, on Broadway, and in motion pictures from 1905 to 1949. Five of the Marx Brothers' thirteen feature films were selected by the American Film Institute (AFI) as among the top 100 comedy films, with two of them (*Duck Soup* and *A Night at the Opera*) in the top twelve. They are widely considered by critics, scholars, and fans to be among the greatest and most influential comedians of the 20th century. The brothers were included in AFI's 100 Years...100 Stars list of the 25 greatest male stars of Classic Hollywood cinema, the only performers to be inducted collectively.

The group are almost universally known today by their stage names: Chico, Harpo, Groucho, Gummo, and Zeppo. The core of the act was the three elder brothers: Chico, Harpo, and Groucho. Each developed a highly distinctive stage persona. Harpo and Chico more or less retired after 1949, while Groucho went on to begin a second career in television. The two younger brothers, Gummo and Zeppo, did not develop their stage characters to the same extent. The two eventually left the act to pursue business careers at which they were successful. They also ran a large theatrical agency for a time, through which they represented their brothers and others. Gummo was not in any of the movies; Zeppo appeared in the first five films in relatively straight (non-comedic) roles. The performing lives of the brothers were brought about by their mother Minnie Marx, who also acted as their manager.

The most popular comedy team of the 1940s and early 1950s was an American comedy duo composed of Bud Abbott and Lou Costello, whose work on radio and in film and television made them international favourites. Their patter routine "Who's on First?" is one of the best-known comedy routines of all time, and set the framework for many of their best-known comedy bits.

In 1940, Universal Studios signed them for a musical, *One Night in the Tropics*. Cast in supporting roles, they stole the show with several classic routines, including the "Who's on First?" routine. Universal signed them to a two-picture contract. Their second film, *Buck Privates* (1941), directed by Arthur Lubin and co-starring The Andrews Sisters, was a massive hit, earning $4 million at the box office and launching Abbott and Costello as stars.

Their next film was a haunted house comedy, *Oh, Charlie!*. However *Buck Privates* was so successful that the studio decided to delay its release so the team could hastily make and release *In The Navy* (1941), co-starring crooner Dick Powell and the Andrews Sisters. This film initially out-grossed *Buck Privates*. *Loew's* Criterion in Manhattan was open until 5 a.m. to oblige over 49,000 customers during the film's first week For a number of years Abbott and Costello were ranked among the most popular stars in the US.

The Three Stooges were an American vaudeville and comedy team active from 1928 until 1970, best known for their 190 Columbia short-subject films that have been airing on television regularly since 1958. Their hallmark was physical farce and slapstick. In films, the Stooges were commonly known by their actual first names. There were a total of six stooges over the act's run, with only three active at any given time, but Moe Howard and Larry Fine were mainstays throughout the ensemble's run of more than forty years.

In 1934, the trio—now officially named "The Three Stooges"—signed on to appear in two-reel comedy short subjects for Columbia Pictures. Moe wrote in his autobiography that they each received $600 per week (equal to $10,742 today) on a one-year contract with a renewable option. In the Ted Okuda–Edward Watz book *The Columbia Comedy Shorts*, the Stooges are said to have received $1,000 among them for their first Columbia effort, *Woman Haters* (1934), and then signed a term contract for $7,500 per film (equal to $134,272 today), to be divided among the trio.

Within their first year at Columbia, the Stooges became very popular. Realizing this, Columbia Pictures president Harry Cohn used the Stooges as leverage, as the demand for their films was so great. He eventually refused to supply exhibitors with the trio's shorts unless they also agreed to book some of the studio's mediocre B movies. Cohn also saw to it that the Stooges remained ignorant of their popularity. During their 23 years at Columbia, the Stooges were never completely aware of their amazing drawing power at the box office. Their contracts with the studio included an open option that had to be renewed yearly. Cohn would tell the boys that the short subjects were in decline, which was not a complete fabrication (Cohn's yearly mantra was, "the market for comedy shorts is dying out, fellas"). The Stooges thought that their days were numbered and would cruelly sweat it out each year, with Cohn renewing their contract at the eleventh hour. This deception kept the insecure Stooges unaware of their true value. This resulted in them having second thoughts about asking for a better contract without a yearly option. Cohn's scare tactic worked for all 23 years that the Stooges were at Columbia. The team never once asked for a salary increase nor were they ever given one. It was not until after they stopped making the shorts in December 1957 that Moe learned of Cohn's underhanded tactics, what a valuable commodity the Stooges had been for the studio and how many millions more the act could have earned.

Chapter 6

The first child star was Shirley Temple (April 23, 1928 – February 10, 2014) actress, singer, dancer, businesswoman, and diplomat who was Hollywood's number one box-office draw as a child actress from 1935 to 1938. As an adult, she was named United States ambassador to Ghana and to Czechoslovakia and also served as Chief of Protocol of the United States.

Temple began her film career at the age of three in 1932. Two years later, she achieved international fame in *Bright Eyes*, a feature film designed specifically for her talents. She received a special Juvenile Academy Award in February 1935 for her outstanding contribution as a juvenile performer in motion pictures during 1934. Film hits such as *Curly Top* and *Heidi* followed year after year during the mid-to-late 1930s. Temple capitalized on licensed merchandise that featured her wholesome image; the merchandise included dolls, dishes, and clothing. Her box-office popularity waned as she reached adolescence. She appeared in a few films of varying quality in her mid-to-late teens, and retired from films in 1950 at the age of 22.

In todays world of political correctness it would be unthinkable for a white performer to wear black make up and sing songs but in days gone by this was perfectly acceptable and the best loved of these was Al Jolson (born Asa Yoelson; May 26, 1886 – October 23, 1950). At the peak of his career, he was dubbed "The World's Greatest Entertainer." His performing style was brash and extroverted, and he popularized a large number of songs that benefited from his "shamelessly sentimental, melodramatic approach." Numerous well-known singers were influenced by his music, including Bing Crosby, David Bowie, Bob Dylan, Rod Stewart and others.

In the 1930s, Jolson was America's most famous and highest-paid entertainer. Between 1911 and 1928, Jolson had nine sell-out Winter Garden shows in a row, more than 80 hit records, and 16 national and international tours. He retired from the stage in 1926 and is best remembered today as the star of the first talking picture, *The Jazz Singer* (1927). He later starred in a series of successful musical films throughout the 1930s. After the attack on Pearl Harbor, he was the first star to entertain troops overseas during World War II. After a period of inactivity, his stardom returned with *The Jolson Story* (1946), for which Larry Parks played Jolson, with the singer dubbing for Parks. The formula was repeated in a sequel, *Jolson Sings Again* (1949). In 1950, he again became the first star to entertain GIs on active service in the Korean War, performing 42 shows in 16 days. He died just weeks after returning to the U.S., partly owing to the physical exertion of performing. Defense Secretary George Marshall posthumously awarded him the Medal of Merit.

Hero of action adventure films was Errol Leslie Flynn (20 June 1909 – 14 October 1959) an Australian-born American actor who achieved fame in Hollywood after 1935. He was known for his romantic swashbuckler roles in Hollywood films, as well as frequent partnerships with Olivia de Havilland. He became a U.S. citizen in 1942.

When Warner Bros were preparing a big budget swashbuckler movie, *Captain Blood* (1935), they decided to cast Flynn in the lead, opposite Olivia de Havilland. The resulting movie was a magnificent success for the studio and Flynn and a new star was launched. The budget for Captain Blood was $1.242 million and it made $3.090 million at the box office thus making Warner Bros. a huge profit.

Public response to *Captain Blood* was so enthusiastic that Warners reunited him with de Havilland in another adventure tale, this time one set in British India, *The Charge of the Light Brigade* (1936). It was another big hit. Flynn followed this with perhaps his most famous movie, *The Adventures of Robin Hood* (1938), playing the title role, opposite de Havilland's Maid Marian. This movie was a world wide success. It was the 6th top movie grosser of 1938. The budget for Robin Hood was the highest ever for a Warner Brothers production up to that point, $2.47 million but it more than made back its costs and turned a huge profit as it grossed $4.838. In England he made another swashbuckler for Warners, *The Master of Ballantrae* (1953). After that Warners ended their contract with him – an association that had lasted for 18 years and 35 films 12 with Olivia de Havilland.

Mary Jane "Mae" West (August 17, 1893 – November 22, 1980) was an American actress, singer, playwright, screenwriter, comedian, and sex symbol whose entertainment career spanned seven decades.

Known for her light-hearted bawdy double entendres, ("why don't you come up and see me sometime?" or "Is that a gun in your pocket or are you just glad to see me?"). With breezy sexual independence, West made a name for herself in vaudeville and on the stage in New York City. She then moved to Hollywood to become a comedian, actress, and writer in the motion picture industry, as well as appearing on radio and television. For her contributions to American cinema, the American Film Institute named West 15th among the greatest female stars of classic American cinema. One of the more controversial movie stars of her day, West encountered many problems, especially censorship. She bucked the system, making comedy out of prudish conventional modes, and the depression-era audience admired her for it. When her cinematic career ended, she wrote books and plays, and continued to perform in Las Vegas, in the United Kingdom, and on radio and television, and to record rock and roll albums. Asked about the various efforts to impede her career, West replied: "I believe in censorship. I made a fortune out of it.". While true, she also suffered greatly because of it, even going to jail for her right to freedom of speech.

In tribute to her statuesque figure air crews nick named their inflatable life preserves Mae Wests.

One man whose screen persona and off screen life merged was W. C. Fields. He was an American comedian, actor, juggler and writer. Fields' comic persona was a misanthropic and hard-drinking egotist, who remained a sympathetic character despite his snarling contempt for dogs and children.

His career in show business began in vaudeville, where he attained international success as a silent juggler. He gradually incorporated comedy into his act, and was a featured comedian in the Ziegfield Follies for several years. He became a star in the Broadway musical comedy *Poppy* (1923), in which he played a colourful small-time con man. His subsequent stage and film roles were often similar scoundrels, or else henpecked everyman characters.

Among his recognizable trademarks were his raspy drawl and grandiloquent vocabulary. The characterization he portrayed in films and on radio was so strong it was generally identified with Fields himself. It was maintained by the publicity departments at Fields' studios (Paramount and Universal) and was further established by Robert Lewis Taylor's biography, *W. C. Fields, His Follies and Fortunes* (1949).In 1973, Fields' grandson, Ronald, published his grandfather's letters, photos and personal notes. They showed that although estranged from his wife, he loved and supported his son and grandchildren.

Fields' screen character often expressed a fondness for alcohol, a prominent component of the Fields legend. Fields never drank in his early career as a juggler, because he did not want to impair his functions while performing. Eventually, the loneliness of constant travel prompted him to keep liquor in his dressing room as an inducement for fellow performers to socialize with him on the road. Only after he became a *Follies* star and abandoned juggling did Fields begin drinking regularly. His role in Paramount Pictures' *International House* (1933), as an aviator with an unquenchable taste for beer, did much to establish Fields' popular reputation as a prodigious drinker. Studio publicists promoted this image, as did Fields himself in press interviews. Fields expressed his fondness for alcohol to Gloria Jean (playing his niece) in *Never Give a Sucker an Even Break*: "I was in love with a beautiful blonde once, dear. She drove me to drink. That's the one thing I am indebted to her for." Equally memorable was a line in the 1940 film *My Little Chickadee*: "Once, on a trek through Afghanistan, we lost our corkscrew...and were compelled to live on food and water for several days." The oft-repeated anecdote that Fields refused to drink water "because fish fuck in it" is unsubstantiated. On movie sets Fields famously shot most of his scenes in varying states of inebriation. During the filming of *Tales of Manhattan*, he kept a vacuum flask with him at all times and frequently availed himself of its contents. In 1936, Fields' heavy drinking precipitated a significant decline in his health. By the following year he recovered sufficiently to make one last film for Paramount, *The Big Broadcast of 1938*, but his troublesome behaviour discouraged other producers from hiring him. By 1938 he was chronically ill, and suffering from delirium tremens.

Over the years Hollywood has turned former professional athletes into film stars with varying degrees of success but none bigger than Johnny Weissmuller (1904-1984). He was an Austro-Hungarian-born American competition swimmer and actor, best known for playing Tarzan in films of the 1930s and 1940s and for having one of the best competitive swimming records of the 20th century. Weissmuller was one of the world's fastest swimmers in the 1920s, winning five Olympic gold medals for swimming and one bronze medal for water polo. He was the first to break the one minute barrier for 100-meter freestyle, and the first to swim 440-yard freestyle under five minutes. He won fifty-two U.S. national championships, set more than 50 world records (spread over both freestyle and backstroke), and was purportedly undefeated in official competition for the entirety of his competitive career. After retiring from competitions, he became the sixth actor to portray Edgar Rice Burroughs's ape man, Tarzan, a role he played in 12 motion pictures. Dozens of other actors have also played Tarzan, but Weissmuller is by far the best known. His character's distinctive Tarzan yell is still often used in films.

While working as an elevator operator and bellboy at the Illinois Athletic Club, Weissmuller caught the eye of swim coach William Bachrach, who trained Weissmuller; In August 1921, Weissmuller won the national championships in the 50-yard and 220-yard distances. Although foreign-born, Weissmuller gave his birthplace as Tanneryville, Cambria County, Pennsylvania, and his birth date as that of his younger brother, Peter Weissmuller. This was to ensure his eligibility to compete as part of the United States Olympic team, and was a critical issue in being issued a United States passport.

His acting career began when he signed a seven-year contract with Metro-Goldwyn-Mayer and played the role of Tarzan in *Tarzan the Ape Man* (1932). The movie was a huge success and Weissmuller became an overnight international sensation. The author of *Tarzan*, Edgar Rice Burroughs, was pleased with Weissmuller,

Weissmuller starred in six Tarzan movies for MGM with actress Maureen O'Sullivan as Jane and Cheeta the Chimpanzee. The last three also included Johnny Sheffield as Boy. Then, in 1942, Weissmuller went to RKO and starred in six more Tarzan movies with markedly reduced production values. Sheffield also appeared as Boy in the first five features for RKO.

Weissmuller earned an estimated $2,000,000 and established himself as what many movie historians consider the definitive Tarzan. Although not the first Tarzan in movies (that was Elmo Lincoln), he was the first to be associated with the now traditional ululating, yodeling Tarzan yell.

When Weissmuller finally left the role of Tarzan, he immediately traded his loincloth costume for a slouch hat and safari suit for the role of *Jungle Jim* (1948) for Columbia. He made thirteen *Jungle Jim* films between 1948 and 1954. According to actor Michael Fox, Weissmuller would shoot two *Jungle Jim* films consecutively with nine days filming for each with a break of two days between, then he would return to his home in Mexico. The following year, he appeared in three more jungle movies, playing himself due to the rights of the name "Jungle Jim" being taken by Screen Gems. He only played three roles in his career. Tarzan, Jungle Jim and himself.

While playing golf in Cuba in 1958 during the Cuban Revolution, Weissmuller's golf cart was suddenly surrounded by rebel soldiers. Weissmuller was unable to communicate who he was until he got out of the cart and attempted the trademark Tarzan yell. The soldiers then recognized him and shouted '"Es Tarzan! Es Tarzan de la Jungla!" Johnny and his companions were not only not kidnapped, but the guerillas gave him an escort to his hotel.

The role of romantic leading actor was filled by Clark Gable (Feb. 1, 1901 – Nov. 16, 1960) film actor and military officer, often referred to as "The King of Hollywood" or just simply as "The King". Gable began his career as a stage actor and appeared as an extra in silent films between 1924 and 1926, and progressed to supporting roles with a few films for Metro-Goldwyn-Mayer in 1931. The next year, he landed his first leading Hollywood role and over the next three decades he became a leading man in more than 60 motion pictures.

Gable won an Academy Award for Best Actor for *It Happened One Night* (1934), and was nominated for leading roles in *Mutiny on the Bounty* (1935) and for his arguably best-known role as Rhett Butler in the epic Civil War drama *Gone with the Wind* (1939). Gable also found success commercially and critically with films such as *Red Dust* (1932), *Manhattan Melodrama* (1934), *San Francisco* (1936), *Saratoga* (1937) *Boom Town* (1940),

The Hucksters (1947), *Homecoming* (1948), and *The Misfits* (1961), which was his final screen appearance. Gable appeared opposite some of the most popular actresses of the time. Joan Crawford was his favourite actress to work with, and she was partnered with Gable in eight films. Myrna Loy worked with him seven times, and he was paired with Jean Harlow in six productions. He also starred with Lana Turner in four features, and with Norma Shearer and Ava Gardner in three each. Gable's final film, *The Misfits* (1961), united him with Marilyn Monroe (also in her last screen appearance). Gable is considered one of the most consistent box-office performers in history, appearing on Quigley Publishing's annual Top Ten Money Making Stars Poll 16 times. He was named the seventh-greatest male star of classic American cinema by the American Film Institute.

The on screen partnership between Spencer Tracy and Katharine Hepburn was one of the most enduring and carried on into their private life.

Spencer Tracy (April 5, 1900 – June 10, 1967) was noted for his natural style and versatility. One of the major stars of Hollywood's Golden Age, Tracy won two Academy Awards for Best Actor, from nine nominations, sharing the record for nominations in that category with Laurence Olivier.

Tracy first discovered his talent for acting while attending Ripon College, and he later received a scholarship for the American Academy of Dramatic Arts. He spent seven years in the theatre, working in a succession of stock companies and intermittently on Broadway. Tracy's breakthrough came in 1930, when his lead performance in *The Last Mile* caught the attention of Hollywood. After a successful film début in *Up the River*, Tracy was signed to a contract with Fox Film Corporation. His five years with Fox were unremarkable, and he remained largely unknown to audiences after 25 films, most of them starring Tracy as the leading man. None of them were hits although *The Power and the Glory* (1933) features one of his most acclaimed performances.

In 1935, Tracy joined Metro-Goldwyn-Mayer, at the time Hollywood's most prestigious studio. His career flourished with a series of hit films, and in 1937 and 1938 he won consecutive Oscars for *Captains Courageous* and *Boys Town*. By the 1940s, Tracy was one of the studio's top stars. In 1942, he appeared with Katharine Hepburn in *Woman of the Year*, beginning a popular partnership that produced nine movies over 25 years. Tracy left MGM in 1955, and continued to work regularly as a freelance star, despite an increasing weariness as he aged. His personal life was troubled, with a lifelong struggle against alcoholism and guilt over his son's deafness. Tracy became estranged from his wife in the 1930s, but never divorced, conducting a long-term relationship with Katharine Hepburn in private. Towards the end of his life, Tracy worked almost exclusively for director Stanley Kramer. It was for Kramer that he made his last film, *Guess Who's Coming to Dinner* in 1967, completed just 17 days before Tracy's death. During his career, Tracy appeared in 75 films and developed a reputation among his peers as one of the screen's greatest actors. In 1999 the American Film Institute ranked Tracy as the 9th greatest male star of Classic Hollywood Cinema.

The other half of the partnership Katharine Hepburn (May 12, 1907– June 29, 2003). Known for her fierce independence and spirited personality, Hepburn was a leading lady in Hollywood for more than 60 years. She appeared in a range of genres, from screwball comedy to literary drama, and she received four Academy Awards—a record for any performer—for Best Actress. In 1999, Hepburn was named by the American Film Institute as the greatest female star of Classic Hollywood Cinema.

Raised in Connecticut by wealthy, progressive parents, Hepburn began to act while studying at Bryn Mawr

College. After four years in the theatre, favourable reviews of her work on Broadway brought her to the attention of Hollywood. Her early years in the film industry were marked with success, including an Academy Award for her third picture, *Morning Glory* (1933), but this was followed by a series of commercial failures that led her to be labeled "box office poison" in 1938. Hepburn masterminded her own comeback, buying out her contract with RKO Radio Pictures and acquiring the film rights to *The Philadelphia Story*, which she sold on the condition that she be the star. In the 1940s, she was contracted to Metro-Goldwyn-Mayer, where her career focused on an alliance with Spencer Tracy. The screen-partnership spanned 25 years and produced nine movies.

Hepburn challenged herself in the latter half of her life, as she regularly appeared in Shakespearean stage productions and tackled a range of literary roles. She found a niche playing middle-aged spinsters, such as in *The African Queen* (1951), a persona the public embraced. Three more Oscars came for her work in *Guess Who's Coming to Dinner* (1967), *The Lion in Winter* (1968), and *On Golden Pond* (1981). In the 1970s, she began appearing in television films, which became the focus of her career in later life. She remained active into old age, making her final screen appearance in 1994 at the age of 87. After a period of inactivity and ill health, Hepburn died in 2003 at the age of 96.Hepburn famously shunned the Hollywood publicity machine and refused to conform to society's expectations of women. She was outspoken, assertive, athletic, and wore trousers before it was fashionable for women to do so. She was briefly married as a young woman, but thereafter lived independently. A 26-year affair with her co-star Spencer Tracy was hidden from the public. With her unconventional lifestyle and the independent characters she brought to the screen, Hepburn epitomized the "modern woman" in the 20th-century United States and is remembered as an important cultural figure.

The role of the Hollywood tough guy was filled with great success by Humphrey Bogart (Dec 25, 1899 – Jan 14, 1957) whose performances in 1940s films noir such as *The Maltese Falcon*, *Casablanca*, and *The Big Sleep* earned him status as a cultural icon.

Bogart began acting in 1921 after a hitch in the U.S. Navy in World War I and little success in various jobs in finance and the production side of the theatre. Gradually he became a regular in Broadway shows in the 1920s and 1930s. When the stock market crash of 1929 reduced the demand for plays, Bogart turned to film. His first great success was as Duke Mantee in *The Petrified Forest* (1936), and this led to a period of typecasting as a gangster with films such as *Angels with Dirty Faces* (1938).

Bogart's breakthrough as a leading man came in 1941 with *High Sierra* and *The Maltese Falcon*. The next year, his performance in *Casablanca* (1943; Oscar nomination) raised him to the peak of his profession and, at the same time, cemented his trademark film persona, that of the hard-boiled cynic who ultimately shows his noble side. Other successes followed, including *To Have and Have Not* (1944), *The Big Sleep* (1946), *Dark Passage* (1947), and *Key Largo* (1948), all four with his wife Lauren Bacall; *The Treasure of the Sierra Madre* (1948); *In a Lonely Place* (1950); *The African Queen* (1951; Oscar winner); *Sabrina* (1954); *The Caine Mutiny* (1954; Oscar nomination); and *We're No Angels* (1955). His last film was *The Harder They Fall* (1956).

During a film career of almost 30 years, Bogart appeared in more than 75 feature films. In 1999, the American Film Institute ranked Bogart as the greatest male star of Classic American cinema. Over his career, he received three Academy Award nominations for Best Actor, winning one (for *The African Queen*).

Another of the Hollywood greats was James "Jimmy" Cagney Jr. (July 17, 1899 – March 30, 1986) actor and dancer, both on stage and in film, though he had his greatest impact in film. Known for his consistently energetic performances, distinctive vocal style, and deadpan comic timing, he won acclaim and major awards for a wide variety of performances. He is best remembered for playing multifaceted tough guys in movies such as *The Public Enemy* (1931), *Taxi!* (1932), *Angels with Dirty Faces* (1938), and *White Heat* (1949), and was typecast or limited by this view earlier in his career. In 1999, the American Film Institute ranked him eighth among its list of greatest male stars of Classic Hollywood Cinema. Orson Welles said of Cagney, "he was maybe the greatest actor who ever appeared in front of a camera". He spent several years in vaudeville as a dancer and comedian, until he got his first major acting part in 1925. He secured several other roles, receiving good notices, before landing the lead in the 1929 play *Penny Arcade*. After rave reviews, Warner Bros. signed him for an initial $500-a-week, three-week contract to reprise his role; this was quickly extended to a seven-year contract.

Cagney's seventh film, *The Public Enemy*, became one of the most influential gangster movies of the period. Notable for a famous scene in which Cagney pushes a grapefruit against Mae Clarke's face, the film thrust him into the spotlight. He became one of Hollywood's biggest stars and one of Warner Bros.' biggest contracts. In 1938, he received his first Academy Award for Best Actor nomination, for *Angels with Dirty Faces*, for his subtle portrayal of the tough guy/man-child Rocky Sullivan. In 1942, Cagney won the Oscar for his energetic portrayal of George M. Cohan in *Yankee Doodle Dandy*. He was nominated a third time in 1955 for *Love Me or Leave Me*. Cagney retired from acting and dancing in 1961 to spend time on his farm with his family. He came out of retirement 20 years later for a part in the movie *Ragtime* (1981), mainly to aid his recovery from a stroke.

Cagney walked out on Warner Bros. several times over the course of his career, each time returning on much improved personal and artistic terms. In 1935, he sued Warner for breach of contract and won. This was one of the first times an actor prevailed over a studio on a contract issue. He worked for an independent film company for a year while the suit was being settled—and established his own production company, Cagney Productions, in 1942, before returning to Warner four years later. Jack L. Warner called him "the Professional Againster". Stanley Kubrick considered him to be one of the best actors of all time. In his first professional acting performance, Cagney danced costumed as a woman in the chorus line of the revue *Every Sailor*, Cagney also made numerous morale-boosting troop tours before and during World War II and was president of the Screen Actors Guild for two years.

The ups and downs of life for a film star are exemplified by Mickey Rooney (born Joseph Yule Jr.; Sep. 23, 1920 – April 6, 2014) an actor, vaudevillian, comedian, producer and radio personality. In a career spanning nine decades and continuing until shortly before his death, he appeared in more than 300 films and was one of the last surviving stars of the silent film era.

At the height of a career that was marked by precipitous declines and raging comebacks, Rooney performed the role of Andy Hardy in a series of 15 films in the 1930s and 1940s that epitomized American family values. A versatile performer, he became a celebrated character actor later in his career. Laurence Olivier once said he considered Rooney "the best there has ever been." Clarence Brown, who directed him in two of his earliest dramatic roles, *National Velvet* and *The Human Comedy*, said he was "the closest thing to a genius I ever worked with."

Rooney first performed in vaudeville as a child and made his film début at the age of six. At 14 he played Puck in the play and later the 1935 film adaptation of *A Midsummer Night's Dream*. Critic David Thomson hailed his performance as "one of cinema's most arresting pieces of magic". In 1938, he co-starred in *Boys Town*. At nineteen he was the first teenager to be nominated for an Oscar for his leading role in *Babes in Arms*, and he was awarded a special Academy Juvenile Award in 1939. At the peak of his career between the ages of 15 and 25, he made forty-three films, which made him one of MGM's most consistently successful actors and a favourite of studio head Louis B. Mayer.

Rooney was the top box office attraction from 1939 to 1941, and one of the best-paid actors of that era, but his career never rose to such heights again. Drafted into the Army during World War II, he served nearly two years entertaining over two million troops on stage and radio and was awarded a Bronze Star for performing in combat zones. Returning from the war in 1945, he was too old for juvenile roles but too short to be an adult movie star, and was unable to get as many starring roles. Nevertheless, Rooney's popularity was renewed with well-received supporting roles in films such as *Requiem for a Heavyweight* (1962), *It's a Mad, Mad, Mad, Mad World* (1963), and *The Black Stallion* (1979). In the early 1980s, he returned to Broadway in *Sugar Babies* and again became a celebrated star. Rooney made hundreds of appearances on TV, including dramas, variety programs, and talk shows, and won an Emmy in 1964, with another Emmy plus a Golden Globe for his role in *Bill* (1981).

At his death, *Vanity Fair* called him "the original Hollywood train wreck." He struggled with alcohol and pill addiction and married eight times, the first time to Ava Gardner. Despite earning millions during his career, he had to file for bankruptcy in 1962 due to mismanagement of his finances. Shortly before his death in 2014 at age 93, he alleged mistreatment by some family members and testified before Congress about what he alleged was physical abuse and exploitation by family members. By the end of his life, his millions in earnings had dwindled to an estate that was valued at only $18,000. He died owing medical bills and back taxes, and contributions were solicited from the public.

One of the best comedy partnerships was that starring Bing Crosby and Bob Hope, KBE, KC*SG, KSS (born Leslie Towns Hope; May 29, 1903 – July 27, 2003) was a multi talented comedian, vaudevillian, actor, singer, dancer, athlete and author. With a career spanning nearly 80 years, Hope appeared in more than 70 short and feature films, including a series of "Road" movies. In addition to hosting the Academy Awards show nineteen times, more than any other host, he appeared in many stage productions and television roles, and was the author of 14 books. The song "Thanks for the Memory" is widely regarded as his signature tune.

Hope was born in Eltham, Kent, England, arrived in America with his family at the age of four, and grew up in the Cleveland, Ohio, area. He began his career in show business in the early 1920s, initially on stage, then began appearing on the radio and in films in 1934. He was praised for his comedy timing, specializing in one-liners and rapid-fire delivery of jokes which often were self-deprecating. Celebrated for his long career performing United Service Organizations (USO) shows to entertain active duty American military personnel—he made 57 tours for the USO between 1941 and 1991—Hope was declared an honorary veteran of the U.S. Armed Forces in 1997 by act of the Congress. He also appeared in numerous specials for NBC television, starting in 1950, and was one of the first users of cue cards. He participated in the sports of golf and boxing and owned a small stake in his home town baseball team, the Cleveland Indians. He died at age 100 at his home in Toluca Lake, California.

In a series of "Road to" pictures he starred in with Bing Crosby he would look at the camera when Crosby was about to sing and tell the audience "time to get the popcorn folks" they remained friends off screen until Crosby's death.

Harry Lillis "Bing" Crosby Jr. (May 3, 1903– Oct 14, 1977).Crosby's trademark warm bass-baritone voice made him the best-selling recording artist of the 20th century, having sold over one billion records, tapes, compact discs and digital downloads around the world.

The first multimedia star, from 1931 to 1954 Crosby was a leader in record sales, radio ratings, and motion picture grosses. His early career coincided with technical recording innovations such as the microphone. This allowed him to develop a laid-back, intimate singing style that influenced many of the popular male singers who followed him, including Perry Como, Frank Sinatra, Dick Haymes, and Dean Martin, *Yank* magazine said that he was the person who had done the most for American soldiers' morale during World War II. In 1948, American polls declared him the "most admired man alive", ahead of Jackie Robinson and Pope Pius XII. Also in 1948, *Music Digest* estimated that his recordings filled more than half of the 80,000 weekly hours allocated to recorded radio music.

Crosby won an Academy Award for Best Actor for his role as Father Chuck O'Malley in the 1944 motion picture *Going My Way* and was nominated for his reprise of the role in *The Bells of St. Mary's* opposite Ingrid Bergman the next year, becoming the first of six actors to be nominated twice for playing the same character. In 1963, Crosby received the first Grammy Global Achievement Award. He is one of 33 people to have three stars on the Hollywood Walk of Fame, in the categories of motion pictures, radio, and audio recording.

Crosby influenced the development of the postwar recording industry. He became the first performer to pre-record his radio shows and master his commercial recordings onto magnetic tape. Through the medium of recording, he constructed his radio programs with the same directorial tools and craftsmanship (editing, retaking, rehearsal, time shifting) used in motion picture production, a practice that became an industry standard. In addition to his work with early tape recording, he helped to finance the development of videotape, bought television stations, bred racehorses, and co-owned the Pittsburgh Pirates baseball team.

The biggest hit song of Crosby's career was his recording of Irving Berlin's *White Christmas*, which he introduced on a Christmas Day radio broadcast in 1941. (A copy of the recording from the radio program is owned by the estate of Bing Crosby and was loaned to *CBS Sunday Morning* for their December 25, 2011, program.) The song then appeared in his 1942 movie *Holiday Inn*. His record hit the charts on October 3, 1942, and rose to No.1 on October 31, where it stayed for 11 weeks. A holiday perennial, the song was repeatedly re-released by Decca, charting another 16 times. It topped the charts again in 1945 and for a third time in January 1947. The song remains the best-selling single of all time. According to *Guinness World Records*, his recording of "White Christmas" has sold over 100 million copies around the world, with at least 50million sales as singles. His recording was so popular that he was obliged to re-record it in 1947 using the same musicians and backup singers; the original 1942 master had become damaged due to its frequent use in pressing additional singles. Though the two versions are similar, the 1947 recording is most familiar today. After his death in 1977, the song was re-released and reached the No. 5 position in the UK Singles Chart in December 1977.Crosby was dismissive of his role in the song's success, saying "a jackdaw with a cleft palate could have sung it successfully.

The pairing of Martin and Lewis was a great success until Martin grew tired of the same plots and ended the partnership.

Dean Martin (born Dino Paul Crocetti; (June 7, 1917 – Dec 25, 1995). One of the most popular and enduring American entertainers of the mid-20th century, Martin was nicknamed the "King of Cool" for his seemingly effortless charisma and self-assurance.

Jerry Lewis and he formed the immensely popular comedy duo Martin and Lewis, with Martin serving as the straight man to Lewis's slapstick, and afterwards he was a member of the "Rat Pack", and a star in concert stages, nightclubs, recordings, motion pictures, and television. He was the host of the television variety program *The Dean Martin Show* and *The Dean Martin Celebrity Roast*.

Martin's relaxed, warbling crooning voice earned him dozens of hit singles, including his signature songs "Memories Are Made of This", "That's Amore", "Ain't That a Kick in the Head?", "You're Nobody Till Somebody Loves You", "Sway", "Volare", Portraying himself as an amiable drunk, in his Las Vegas shows he would be introduced as "and now straight from the bar Dean Martin".

Jerry Lewis (March 16, 1926 – August 20, 2017) was an American comedian, actor, singer, producer, director, screenwriter, and humanitarian.

He was known for his slapstick humour in film, television, stage and radio. From 1946 to 1956, he and Dean Martin were partners as the hit popular comedy duo of Martin and Lewis. From then on, he became a solo star in motion pictures, nightclubs, television shows, concerts, album recordings and musicals.

Lewis served as national chairman of the Muscular Dystrophy Association and hosted the live Labor Day weekend broadcast of the *Jerry Lewis MDA Telethon* for 45 years.

He received several awards for lifetime achievement from the American Comedy Awards, Los Angeles Film Critics Association, Venice Film Festival and Academy of Motion Picture Arts and Sciences, and was honoured with two stars on the Hollywood Walk of Fame. The duo began their Paramount film careers as ensemble players in *My Friend Irma* (1949), based on the popular radio series of the same name. This was followed by a sequel *My Friend*

Irma Goes West (1950). Starting with *At War with the Army* (1950), Martin and Lewis were the stars of their own vehicles in fourteen additional titles, *That's My Boy* (1951), *Sailor Beware* (1952), *Jumping Jacks* (1952; also appearing in the Crosby and Hope film, *Road to Bali* as cameos), *The Stooge* (1952), *Scared Stiff* (1953), *The Caddy* (1953), *Money from Home* (1953), *Living It Up* (1954), *3 Ring Circus* (1954), *You're Never Too Young* (1955), *Artists and Models* (1955) and *Pardners* (1956) at Paramount, ending with *Hollywood or Bust* (1956).

All sixteen movies were produced by Hal B. Wallis.

It was not always humans that were the stars, two of the biggest were dogs.

Rin Tin Tin (often hyphenated as Rin-Tin-Tin; Sep. 1918 – Aug. 10, 1932) was a male German Shepherd that was an international star in motion pictures. He was rescued from a World War I battlefield by an American soldier, who nicknamed him "Rinty".Following advances made by American forces during the Battle of Saint-Mihiel, Corporal Lee Duncan, an aerial gunner of the U.S. Army Air Service, was sent forward on September 15, 1918, to the small French village of Flirey to see if it would make a suitable flying field for his unit, the 135th Aero Squadron. The area had been subject to bombs and artillery, and Duncan found a severely damaged kennel which had once supplied the Imperial German Army with German Shepherd dogs. The only dogs left alive in the kennel were a starving mother with a litter of five nursing puppies, their eyes still shut because they were less than a week old. Duncan rescued the dogs and brought them back to his unit. When the puppies were weaned, he gave the mother to an officer and three of the litter to other soldiers, but he kept a male and a female. Duncan trained Rin Tin Tin and obtained silent film work for the dog. Rin Tin Tin was an immediate box-office success and went on to appear in 27 Hollywood films, gaining worldwide fame. Along with the earlier canine film star Strongheart, Rin

Tin Tin was responsible for greatly increasing the popularity of German Shepherd dogs as family pets. The immense profitability of his films contributed to the success of studios, and helped advance the career of Darryl F. Zanuck.

The other canine star was a breed of dog known as a rough collie named Pal who starred in Lassie Come Home the first of seven films featuring Pal. The story being, during the depression the family sell their sons pet who travels hundreds of miles to be reunited with the boy, the film also starred a young Elisabeth Taylor.

Chapter 7

The Golden age of Hollywood musicals was the 1930's-1950's. In that time the partnership of Fred Astaire and Ginger Rogers stands supreme.

Fred Astaire (May 10, 1899- June 22, 1987) and Ginger Rogers (July 16, 1911- April 25, 1995) were iconic dance partners who made motion pictures together from 1933–1949. They made a total of 10 movies, 9 with RKO Radio Pictures and one, *The Barkleys of Broadway*, with M-G-M, their only colour (Technicolor) movie.

Astaire started dancing in the early 1900s as a child on stage, in Vaudeville, partnering with his older sister, Adele. He made his first movie in 1933, taking on a small role in the movie *Dancing Lady* starring Clark Gable and Joan Crawford. Rogers made her first appearance in a 1929 movie short, then made feature Pre-Code movies with Warner Brothers Pictures such as *42nd Street* and *Gold Diggers of 1933*. Astaire and Rogers made their first pairing in a movie in 1933, *Flying Down to Rio*, in which they had supporting roles; the main star was Dolores Del Rio. In 1934, Astaire and Rogers made the musical movie *The Gay Divorcee* which co-starred Edward Everett Horton; it was their first joint starring role in a movie; the movie also featured the classic Cole Porter song "Night and Day". The song "The Continental" from the movie was a hit and was also the first song to win the Academy Award for Best Original Song in the 1934 Academy Awards.

The other great star in this genre was Gene Kelly (Aug 23, 1912 – Feb 2, 1996) a dancer, actor of film, stage and television, singer, film director, producer, and choreographer. He was known for his energetic and athletic dancing style, his good looks, and the likeable characters that he played on screen. Best known today for his performances in films such as *American in Paris* (1951), *Anchors Aweigh* (1945), and *Singin' in the Rain*

(1952), he starred in musical films until they fell out of fashion in the late 1950s. He starred in many musical films throughout the 1940s, including *For Me and My Gal* (1942), *Du Barry Was A Lady* (1943), *Thousands Cheer* (1943), and *On the Town* (1949). He starred as the lead in the film *It's Always Fair Weather* (1955) which has gained a cult following among musical enthusiasts and his fans. In his later career, he starred in two films outside the musical genre: *Inherit the Wind* (1960) and *What a Way to Go!* (1964). Throughout his career, he also directed films (some of which he starred in), most notably the 1969 film *Hello, Dolly!*,which was nominated for the Academy Award for Best Picture. During filming of *Anchors Aweigh* one of the other stars, Frank Sinatra, spent eight weeks learning the opening dance routine. When filming the scene it took seventy four takes before musical director Kelly was satisfied, Sinatra later stated he could have made an entire film in eight weeks, the pair never spoke again, Also in the film was a dance routine that was innovative at the time, a mixture of live action and animation. Kelly approached Walt Disney for permission to use Mickey Mouse but Disney refused so he turned to M.G.M. for Jerry from the Tom and Jerry cartoons. They agreed and the three minute sequence took two months and cost $100,000 to make, when finished Kelly noticed that when dancing his shadow was on the floor but Jerry's was not so the animators had to go through over a 100,000 drawings and put in a shadow. His many innovations transformed the Hollywood musical and he is credited with almost single-handedly making the ballet form commercially acceptable to film audiences. Kelly received an Academy Honorary Award in 1952 for his career achievements. He later received lifetime achievement awards in the Kennedy Center Honors (1982), and from the Screen Actors Guild and American Film Institute. In 1999, the American Film Institute also numbered him 15th in their Greatest Male Stars of Classic Hollywood cinema list.

Through the 1950's-60's Doris Day (born Doris Mary Ann Kappelhoff; April 3, 1922 -May 13 2019) was the biggest female box office star. She began her career as a big band singer in 1939, her popularity increased with her first hit recording "Sentimental Journey" (1945). After leaving Les Brown & His Band of Renown to embark on a solo career, she recorded more than 650 songs from 1947 to 1967, which made her one of the most popular and acclaimed singers of the 20th century. Day's film career began with the 1948 film *Romance on the High Seas*, and its success sparked her twenty-year career as a motion picture actress. She starred in a series of successful films, including musicals, comedies, and dramas. She played the title role in *Calamity Jane* (1953), and starred in Alfred Hitchcock's *The Man Who Knew Too Much* (1956) with James Stewart. Her most successful films were the "pioneering" bedroom comedies she made co-starring Rock Hudson and James Garner, such as *Pillow Talk* (1959) and *Move Over, Darling* (1963), respectively. She also co-starred in films with such leading men as Clark Gable, Cary Grant, David Niven, and Rod Taylor. After her final film in 1968, she went on to star in the CBS sitcom *The Doris Day Show* (1968–73). She was usually one of the top ten singers between 1951 and 1966. As an actress, she became the biggest female film star in the early 1960s, and ranked sixth among the box office performers by 2012. In 2011, she released her 29th studio album, *My Heart*, which became a UK Top 10 album featuring new material. Among her awards, Day has received the Grammy Lifetime Achievement Award and a Legend Award from the Society of Singers. In 1960, she was nominated for the Academy Award for Best Actress, and in 1989 was given the Cecil B. DeMille Award for lifetime achievement in motion pictures. In 2004, she was awarded the Presidential Medal of Freedom by President George W. Bush followed in 2011 by the Los Angeles Film Critics Association's Career Achievement Award She died in 2019.

The part of the suave, sophisticated leading man was firmly established as his own by Cary Grant (born Archibald Alec Leach; Jan 18, 1904– Nov 29, 1986) a British-American actor, known as one of classic Hollywood's definitive leading men. He began a career in Hollywood in the early 1930s, and became known for his transatlantic accent, debonair demeanor, and light-hearted approach to acting and sense of comic timing. He became an American citizen in 1942 having established himself as a major Hollywood star, he was nominated twice for the Academy Award for Best Actor, for *Penny Serenade* (1941) and *None but the Lonely Heart* (1944).

In the 1940s and 1950s, Grant forged a working relationship with the director Alfred Hitchcock, appearing in films such as *Suspicion* (1941), *Notorious* (1946), *To Catch a Thief* (1955) and *North by Northwest* (1959). Hitchcock admired Grant and considered him to have been the only actor that he had ever loved working with. Towards the end of his film career, Grant was praised by critics as a romantic leading man, and received five Golden Globe Award for Best Actor nominations, including *Indiscreet* (1958) with Ingrid Bergman, *That Touch of Mink* (1962) with Doris Day, and *Charade* (1963) with Audrey Hepburn. He is remembered by critics for his unusually broad appeal, as a handsome, suave actor who did not take himself too seriously, possessing the ability to play with his own dignity in comedies without sacrificing it entirely. His comic timing and delivery made Grant what *Premiere* magazine considers to have been "quite simply, the funniest actor cinema has ever produced."

In war movies actors playing the part were often not fit enough to be part of active military service but one man who made the transition was Audie Leon Murphy (20 June 1925 – 28 May 1971). He was one of the most decorated American combat soldiers of World War II, receiving every military combat award for valor available from the U.S. Army, as well as French and Belgian awards for heroism. Murphy received the Medal of Honor for valor demonstrated at the age of 19 for single-handedly holding off an entire company of German soldiers for an hour at the Colmar Pocket in France in January 1945, then leading a successful counter-attack while wounded and out of ammunition.

Murphy was born into a large sharecropper family in Hunt County, Texas. His father abandoned them, and his mother died when he was a teenager. Murphy left school in fifth grade to pick cotton and find other work to help support his family; his skill with a hunting rifle was a necessity for putting food on the table.

After the attack on Pearl Harbor, Murphy's older sister helped him to falsify documentation about his birth date to meet the minimum-age requirement for enlisting in the military. Turned down by the Navy and the Marine Corps, he enlisted in the Army. He first saw action in the Allied Invasion of Sicily and the Battle of Anzio, and in 1944 participated in the liberation of Rome and invasion of southern France. Murphy fought at Montélimar, and led his men on a successful assault at the L'Omet quarry near Cleurie in north-eastern France in October.

After the war, Murphy enjoyed a 21-year acting career. He played himself in the 1955 autobiographical film *To Hell and Back*, based on his 1949 memoirs of the same name, but most of his roles were in westerns. He made guest appearances on celebrity television shows and starred in the series *Whispering Smith*. Murphy was a fairly accomplished songwriter, and bred quarter horses in California and Arizona, becoming a regular participant in horse racing.

Suffering from what would today be termed posttraumatic stress disorder (PTSD), he slept with a loaded handgun under his pillow and looked for solace in addictive sleeping pills. In his last few years, he was plagued by money problems, but refused offers to appear in alcohol and cigarette commercials because he did not want to set a bad example. Murphy died in a plane crash in Virginia in 1971 shortly before his 46th birthday, and was interred with full military honours at Arlington National Cemetery. His grave is the second most visited after president John F Kennedy's and because of the number of visitors a special path was laid to prevent damage.

Chapter 8

Before the advent of television the only way to see news events or sporting moments was to go to the cinema where between features was a news item lasting about five minutes, Pathé News was a producer of newsreels and documentaries from 1910 until 1970 in the United Kingdom. Its founder, Charles Pathé, was a pioneer of moving pictures in the silent era. The Pathé News archive is known today as British Pathé. Its collection of news film and movies is fully digitized and available online.

Its roots lie in 1896 Paris, France, when Société Pathé Frères was founded by Charles Pathé and his brothers, who pioneered the development of the moving image. Charles Pathé adopted the national emblem of France, the cockerel, as the trademark for his company.

On this side of the Atlantic the golden era of film production was post war making what are now regarded as classics. Not having the lavish budgets of Hollywood studios the British film industry still managed to produce memorable films, among the best was from the Rank Organization, a British entertainment conglomerate founded by industrialist J. Arthur Rank in April 1937. It quickly became the largest and most vertically integrated film company in Britain, owning production, distribution and exhibition facilities. It also diversified into the manufacture of radios, TVs and photocopiers (as one of the owners of Rank Xerox). The company name lasted until February 1996 when the name and some of the remaining assets were absorbed into the newly structured the Rank Group Plc.

J. Arthur Rank, born in Kingston upon Hull, UK, was already a wealthy industrialist through his father's flour milling business, Joseph Rank Ltd, when he made his somewhat unlikely start in film-making, financing short religious subjects in line with his Methodist beliefs. From these modest origins, the British film company emerged in 1937 as Rank sought to consolidate his film-making interests.

The company logo, the Gongman, first used in 1935 by the group's distribution company General Film Distributors and seen in the opening titles of the films, became a celebrated and enduring film emblem.

The Gongman (also known as the "man-with-the-gong") is a company trademark for the Rank Organisation. It was used as the introduction to all Rank films, many of which were shot at their Pinewood Studios, and included those which Rank distributed. The Gongman logo was first used on films distributed by General Film Distributors, which was established in 1935 by the British producer C. M. Woolf and J. Arthur Rank; it was C.M. Woolf's secretary who devised the man-with-a-gong trademark. When the Rank Organization was established in 1937, with General Film Distributors as one of its cornerstones, the logo was adopted for the whole organization.

Athletes who played the Gongman in the film sequence over the years, included boxer Bombardier Billy Wells and wrestler Ken Richmond.

Ealing Studios is a television and film production company and facilities provider at Ealing Green in west London. Will Barker bought the White Lodge on Ealing Green in 1902 as a base for film making, and films have been made on the site ever since. It is the oldest continuously working studio facility for film production in the world, and the current stages were opened for the use of sound in 1931. It is best known for a series of classic films produced in the post-WWII years, including *Kind Hearts and Coronets* (1949), *Passport to Pimlico* (1949), *The Lavender Hill Mob* (1951), and *The Ladykillers* (1955). The BBC owned and filmed at the Studios for forty years from 1955 until 1995. Since 2000, Ealing Studios has resumed releasing films under its own name, including the revived *St Trinian's* franchise. In more recent times, films shot here include *The Importance of Being*

Earnest (2002) and *Shaun of the Dead* (2004), as well as *The Theory of Everything* (2014), *The Imitation Game* (2014) and *Burnt* (2015). Interior scenes of the British period drama television series *Downton Abbey* were shot in Stage 2 of the studios. The Met Film School London operates on the site.

One of the brightest female stars of the British film Industry was Gracie Fields who was born over a fish and chip shop owned by her grandmother, in Molesworth Street, Rochdale, Lancashire. She made her first stage appearance as a child in 1905, joining children's repertory theatre groups such as 'Haley's Garden of Girls' and the 'Nine Dainty Dots'. Her two sisters, Edith and Betty and brother, Tommy, all went on to appear on stage, but Gracie was the most successful. Her professional début in variety took place at the Rochdale Hippodrome theatre in 1910 and she soon gave up her job in the local cotton mill, where she was a half-timer, spending half a week in the mill and the other half at school.

Fields came to major public notice in *Mr Tower of London*, which appeared in London's West End. Her career accelerated from this point with legitimate dramatic performances and the beginning of a successful recording career.

At one point, Fields was playing three shows a night in London's West End. She appeared in the Pitt production *SOS* with Gerald Du Maurier, a legitimate production staged at the St James's Theatre.

Fields' most famous song, which became her theme, "Sally", was worked into the title of her first film, *Sally in Our Alley* (1931), which was a major box office hit. She went on to make several films initially in Britain and later in the United States (for which she was paid a record fee of £200,000 for four films). Regardless, she never enjoyed performing without a live audience, and found the process of film-making boring.

During the 1930's and 40's the most popular entertainer was George Formby, OBE (born George Hoy Booth; 26

May 1904 – 6 March 1961), singer-songwriter and comedian who became known to a worldwide audience through his films of the 1930s and 1940s. On stage, screen and record he sang light, comical songs, usually playing the ukulele or banjolele, and became the UK's highest-paid entertainer. Born in Wigan, Lancashire, he was the son of George Formby Sr, from whom he later took his stage name. After an early career as a stable boy and jockey, Formby took to the music hall stage after the early death of his father in 1921. His early performances were taken exclusively from his father's act, including the same songs, jokes and characters. In 1923 he made two career-changing decisions – he purchased a ukulele, and married Beryl Ingham a fellow performer who became his manager and transformed his act. She insisted that he appear on stage formally dressed, and introduced the ukulele to his performance. He started his recording career in 1926 and, from 1934, he increasingly worked in film to develop into a major star by the late 1930s and 1940s, and became the UK's most popular entertainer during those decades. The media historian Brian McFarlane writes that on film, Formby portrayed gormless Lancastrian innocents who would win through against some form of villainy, gaining the affection of an attractive middle-class girl in the process.

During the Second World War Formby worked extensively for the Entertainments National Service Association (ENSA), and entertained civilians and troops, and by 1946 it was estimated that he had performed in front of three million service personnel. After the war his career declined, although he toured the Commonwealth, and continued to appear in variety and pantomime. His last television appearance was in December 1960, two weeks before the death of Beryl. He surprised people by announcing his engagement to a school teacher seven weeks after Beryl's funeral, but died in Preston three weeks later, at the age of 56; he was buried in Warrington, alongside his father.

Playing the part of a pompous incompetent figure of authority Will Hay FRAS (6 December 1888 – 18 April 1949) comedian, actor, author, film director and amateur astronomer came to notice for his theatrical sketch as a jocular schoolmaster, known as Dr. Muffin. The acts in which Hay performed the schoolmaster sketch became known as "The Fourth Form at St. Michael's". Hay toured with his act and appeared in America, Canada, Australia and South Africa. From 1934 to 1943, he was a prolific film star in Britain, and was ranked the third highest grossing star at the British Box Office in 1938, behind George Formby and Gracie Fields. Hay worked with Gainsborough Pictures from 1935 to 1940, during which time he developed a partnership with Graham Moffatt, an insolent overweight schoolboy, and Moore Marriott, a toothless old man. Hay's 1937 film, with Moffatt and Marriott, *Oh, Mr. Porter!* was credited by *The Times* as being "a comic masterpiece of the British cinema", while the writer, Jimmy Perry, cited the film as an influence for developing the key characters in *Dad's Army*. Hay often portrayed incompetent authority figures who attempted to conceal their incompetence but whose true traits were exposed by those around him. As well as being incompetent, his characters are often immoral, such as his portrayal of a vicar involved in horse betting in *Dandy Dick*, a fraudster who lies about his career as a distinguished sea captain in *Windbag the Sailor.* He also played a prison warden, Dr Benjamin Twist, in *Convict 99* who obtains his job by false pretenses. He is often compared to W. C. Fields, who portrayed characters similar to that of Hay, often being misanthropic, self-centered scoundrels who still remained sympathetic despite their characteristics. Hay was also an amateur astronomer, and in 1933 gained fame for discovering a Great White Spot on Saturn. He built his own observatory, and was a Fellow of the Royal Astronomical Society.

Old Mother Riley was a music hall act which made a successful transition from stage to silver screen,

It originally ran from about 1934 to 1954 played by Arthur Lucan, and from 1954 to the 1980s played by Roy Rolland.

Old Mother Riley was an Irish washerwoman and charwoman character, devised by Lucan (born Arthur Towle). His wife Kitty McShane played Old Mother Riley's daughter, Kitty. It was essentially a drag act but also a double act. The couple played music halls, theatres, and broadcast on radio and appeared in films. Lucan was voted sixth biggest British box-office star by the *Motion Picture Herald* in 1943. They also gave Jimmy Clitheroe his break in 1939 in an Old Mother Riley pantomime called *The Old Woman who Lives in a Shoe*, and then the following year a part in their film, *Old Mother Riley in Society*. The *Film Fun* comic included an "Old Mother Riley" strip cartoon in the 1940s.

Roy Rolland was Lucan's understudy and stand-in, and after Lucan's death in 1954 he continued to play the Old Mother Riley character in pantomime, on television and in cabaret until the 1980s.

Made on a minuscule budget, but extremely profitable, 15 of the 17 films made by Arthur Lucan featured him as Old Mother Riley.

Alistair Sim (1900-1976) Born on Lothian Road where there is a plaque commemorating him outside the Film House. After serving in WW1 he became a lecturer at Edinburgh University before moving to London and joining the Old Vic Company. During the late 40's and the 50's he was a leading star of over fifty films most notably *An Inspector Calls, The Green Man* and *Scrooge* considered by many to be the best on screen portrayal of a title character. It was his role in *The Belles of St. Trinians* that is probably best remembered. He signed up to play Clarence Fritton when it was discovered Margaret Rutherford was unavailable to play Millicent Fritton so Sim played both roles, one in drag.

The film was the biggest box office success of 1954.

He was very guarded about his private life never giving interviews or signing autographs but he was very supportive of young actors many of whom lived in his house. One in particular, was George Cole (Arfur in the T.V. series Minder) who lived with the family for twelve years before getting married and buying a house nearby.

The school St. Trinians was based on a real school of the same name opened by Miss Catherine Fraser-Lee in 1922 on Palmerston Road. The school moved to St. Leonards House, now part of Pollock Halls which is now student accommodation. In 1925 Miss Fraser Lee based the school curriculum on the Dalton system of education where the pupils were largely responsible for their own progress with senior pupils not the staff making the rules and deciding what punishments should be. This style gained the school a reputation of "they do what they like". Her attitude was that other schools sent their pupils out into the world totally unprepared whereas she sent her pupils out into a world that was totally unprepared for them.

During WW11a young soldier, Ronald Searle visited friends whose daughters attended the school and they told him about the way the school was run, he drew a series of humorous cartoons depicting his take on school life with the fourth formers feral little girls causing mayhem on the hockey field and the sixth formers wearing make -up high heels and short skirts distilling gin in the science lab and figuring the odds on horse racing in the maths room. These cartoons were published in Lilliput magazine and were an instant hit. Ronald Searle rejoined his regiment and was captured by the Japanese at the fall of Singapore and sent to work on the death railway were he kept drawing the dreadful conditions that he saw on a daily basis. The Japanese guards caught him and took him to the parade ground where they smashed his right hand with a rifle butt not knowing he was left handed. After the war he submitted many more drawings to the magazine and the British film industry made them into four films.

Sir Norman Joseph Wisdom, OBE (4 Feb. 1915 – 4 Oct. 2010) English actor, comedian, and singer-songwriter best known for a series of comedy films produced between 1953 and 1966 featuring his hapless on-screen character that was often called Norman Pitkin. He was awarded the 1953 BAFTA Award for Most Promising Newcomer to Leading Film Roles following the release of *Trouble in Store*, his first film in a lead role.

Wisdom gained celebrity status in lands as far apart as South America, Iran and many Eastern Bloc countries, particularly in Albania where his films were the only ones by Western actors permitted by dictator Enver Hoxha to be shown. Charlie Chaplin once referred to Wisdom as his "favourite clown".

Wisdom later forged a career on Broadway in New York and as a television actor, winning critical acclaim for his dramatic role of a dying cancer patient in the television play *Going Gently* in 1981. He toured Australia and South Africa. After the 1986 Chernobyl disaster, a hospice was named in his honour. In 1995 he was given the Freedom of the City of London and of Tirana. The same year he received an OBE.

Wisdom was knighted in 2000 and spent much of his later life on the Isle of Man. His later appearances included television roles in *Last of the Summer Wine* and *Coronation Street*, and he retired from acting at the age of 90 after his health deteriorated. He died on 4 October 2010, at age 95.

Among the actors playing serious roles was Sir Alec Guinness, CH CBE (born Alec Guinness de Cuffe, 2 April 1914 – 5 Aug. 2000). After an early career on the stage, Guinness was featured in several of the Ealing Comedies, including *The Ladykillers* and *Kind Hearts and Coronets* in which he played nine different characters. He is also known for his six collaborations with David Lean: Herbert Pocket in *Great Expectations* (1946), Fagin in *Oliver Twist* (1948), Col. Nicholson in *The Bridge On the River Kwai* (1957, for which he won the Academy Award for Best

Actor), Prince Faisal in *Lawrence of Arabia* (1962), General Yevgraf Zhivago in *Doctor Zhivago* (1965), and Professor Godbole in *A Passage to India* (1984). He is also known for his portrayal of Obi-Wan Kenobi in George Lucas's original *Star Wars* trilogy, receiving a nomination for an Academy Award for Best Supporting Actor. Guinness was one of three British actors, along with Laurence Olivier and John Gielgud, who made the transition from Shakespearean theatre to blockbuster films immediately after World War II. Guinness served in the Royal Naval Reserve during the war and commanded a landing craft during the invasion of Sicily and Elba. During the war he was granted leave to appear in the stage play *Flare Path* about the RAF Bomber Command.

Guinness won an Academy Award, a BAFTA, a Golden Globe and a Tony Award. In 1959, he was knighted by Queen Elizabeth II for services to the arts. He received a star on the Hollywood Walk of Fame in 1960, the Academy Honorary Award for lifetime achievement in 1980 and the BAFTA Academy Fellowship Award in 1989.

Dirk Bogarde (born Derek Jules Gaspard Ulric Niven van den Bogaerde; 28 March 1921 – 8 May 1999). Initially a matinée idol in films such as *Doctor in the House* (1954) for the Rank Organisation, he later acted in art-house films. In a second career, he wrote seven best-selling volumes of memoirs, six novels and a volume of collected journalism, mainly from articles in *The Daily Telegraph*.

Bogarde came to prominence in films including *The Blue Lamp* in the early 1950s, before starring in the successful *Doctor* film series (1954–63). He twice won the BAFTA Award for Best Actor in a Leading Role; for *The Servant* (1963) and *Darling* (1965). His other notable film roles included *Victim* (1961), *Accident* (1967), *The Damned* (1969), *Death in Venice* (1971), *The Night Porter* (1974), A Bridge Too Far (1977) and *Despair* (1978). He was appointed a Commander of the Order of Arts and Letters in 1990 and a Knight Bachelor in 1992.

James Robertson Justice (born James Norval Harald Justice, 15 June 1907 – 2 July 1975) was an English character actor who appeared in British films during the 1940s, 1950s 1960's Justice was the demanding surgeon Sir Lancelot Spratt in the "Doctor" series of films of the 1950s and 1960s, beginning with *Doctor in the House* (1954), playing a role for which he is possibly best remembered.

The son of an Aberdeen-born geologist and named after his father, James Robertson Justice was born James Norval Harald Justice in Lee, a suburb of Lewisham in South London, in 1907. Educated at Marlborough College in Wiltshire, Justice studied science at University College London, but left after a year and became a geology student at the University of Bonn, where he again left after just a year. He spoke many languages (possibly up to 20) including Spanish, French, Greek, Danish, Russian, German, Italian, Dutch and Gaelic.

Richard Andrew Palethorpe Todd OBE (11 June 1919 – 3 December 2009) was an Irish-born British soldier and stage and film actor. At the beginning of World War II Todd enlisted into the British Army, receiving a commission in 1941. Initially, he served in the King's Own Yorkshire Light Infantry (KOYLI) before joining the Parachute Regiment, being assigned to the 7th (Light Infantry) Parachute Battalion as part of the British 6th Airborne Division.

On 6 June 1944, as a captain, he participated in Operation Tonga during the D-Day landings. Todd was among the first British officers to land in Normandy as part of Operation Overlord. His Battalion parachuted in after the initial glider-borne forces had landed with the objective of capturing the Pegasus Bridge near Caen. During the operation he met Major John Howard on the bridge, and organized the repelling of several German counter-attacks.

As an actor Todd would later play Major Howard in the film *The Longest Day*, recreating these events for a cinema production.

Sir John Mills, CBE (born Lewis Ernest Watts Mills, 22 February 1908 – 23 April 2005) was an English actor who appeared in more than 120 films in a career spanning seven decades. On screen, he often played people who are not at all exceptional, but become heroes because of their common sense, generosity and good judgment. He received an Academy Award for Best Supporting Actor for his work in *Ryan's Daughter*.

Diana Dors (born Diana Mary Fluck; 23 October 1931 – 4 May 1984). She first came to public notice as a blonde bombshell in the style of American Marilyn Monroe, as promoted by her first husband, Dennis Hamilton, mostly via sex film-comedies and risqué modeling. When it turned out that Hamilton had been defrauding her for his own benefit, she had little choice but to play up to her established image, and she made tabloid headlines with the adult parties reportedly held at her house. Later, she showed a genuine talent for TV, recordings, and cabaret, and gained new popularity as a regular chat-show guest.

Dors claimed to have left a large fortune to her son in her will, via a secret code in the possession of her third husband, actor Alan Lake, but after Lake's suicide, this code was never found, and the whereabouts of the fortune remains a mystery.

Jack Hawkins, CBE (14 Sep. 1910 – 18 July 1973) was an English actor who worked on stage and in film from the 1930s until the 1970s. One of the most popular British film stars of the 1950's, he was best known for his portrayal of military men in films like, *Angels One Five* (1951), *The Cruel Sea* (1953), *Bridge on the River Kwai* (1957), *Ben Hur* (1959) and *Lawrence of Arabia* (1962).

Richard Attenborough, Baron Attenborough, CBE 29 Aug. 1923– 24 Aug. 2014) was an actor, filmmaker, entrepreneur, and politician. He was the President of the Royal Academy of Dramatic Art (RADA) and the British Academy of Film and Television Arts (BAFTA). Attenborough joined the Royal Air Force during World War II and served in the film unit. He went on several bombing raids over Europe and filmed action from the rear gunner's position.

As a film director and producer, Attenborough won two Academy Awards for *Gandhi* in 1983. He also won four BAFTA Awards and four Golden Globe Awards. As an actor, he is perhaps best known for his roles in *Brighton Rock*, *The Great Escape*, *10 Rillington Place*, *Miracle on 34th Street* (1994) and *Jurassic Park*.

He was the older brother of David Attenborough, a naturalist and broadcaster, and John Attenborough, an executive at Alfa Romeo. He was married to actress Sheila Sim from 1945 until his death.

Theatres

Chapter 9

Like the cinemas the variety theatres suffered with the advent of television. These shows were a mixture of singing, dancing and humour. With two shows a night and a matinee on a Saturday it was a tough life for the performers especially during the second house when the audience had a few libations and were known to be raucous. The comedian was king with star names such as Johnny Victory son of Peter Victory a local cabbie, Hector Nichol a local man with a line in risque patter, Lex MacLean from Glasgow whose shows at the Palladium were always a sell out, and one man who many people thought the best, from Greenock, Chic Murray with his wife Maidie, billed as the Tall Droll with the Small Doll they were a double act she playing accordion, he singing and making remarks about her.

Later, working as a solo act, with a forbidding expression and wearing a bunnet Murray offered a comic vision of the world that was absurd and surreal, "I was walking along the road when a car stopped and the driver asked if I wanted a lift, I replied, "no thanks I live in a bungalow".

He owned a hotel in Bruntsfield Crescent until his death in 1985. In 2005 he was voted the comedians comedian by his peers.

The Empire Palace on Nicholson Street was the scene of a major tragedy in 1911 when it was destroyed by fire. Appearing there was the Great Lafayette the illusionist and the highest paid performer of his time earning an estimated £24,000 a year. His dog Beauty, a gift from Harry Houdini had led a pampered life eating five meals a day and wearing a diamond encrusted collar, died. A bereft

Lafayette made an arrangement with the council for the dog to be buried in Piershill cemetery on condition that when he died he would be buried in the same plot. Four days later during his show whilst doing the illusion "lion lady" in which he appeared to turn a lion into a lady, faulty lights caught fire and the set was destroyed in minutes. The audience did not move thinking this was part of the act, it was not until the theatre manager played God Save The King that they exited the building. Ten members of the cast trapped behind a jammed safety curtain perished including Lafayette. The theatre was completely destroyed and the body of Lafayette was apparently found and sent to Glasgow for cremation. Two days later workmen discovered a second body identically dressed. The first body turned out to be his double. On 14th May Lafayette's ashes were taken to Piershill cemetery witnessed by 250,000 onlookers where his urn was laid to rest between the paws of Beauty.

The theatre was rebuilt in three months and would go on to host the top names in the entertainment business including Laurel and Hardy. The inevitable happened in 1963, when it changed to a bingo hall. In 1994 after major refurbishment it reopened as the Festival Theatre home to opera, ballet and musical theatre.

The Palladium on East Fountainbridge began life as a cinema in 1911 but was converted to a theatre in 1932, and into a variety theatre in 1935. A host of big names played there including the Alexander Brothers, Welsh crooner Donald Peers and the always popular Lex MacLean. The theatre closed in 1966 and became a bingo hall for a few years before becoming the White Elephant nightclub later Valentinos before being demolished in 1984.

With the demise of the Variety theatre many entertainers switched to the booming social club scene.

One of the most popular street entertainers was Mrs Dunlop and her pony Smokey who pulled a barrel organ round the streets of the West End and as far as

Morningside from the 1930's to the 1960's. For a while she had a monkey that would dance to the tunes and this led to her being known as Monkey Mary. When she died in 1966 Smokey went to the S.S.P.C.A. sanctuary at Balerno and the barrel organ is on show in the Childrens Museum on the High Street.

Radio

Chapter 10

Before the days of mass ownership of cars very few people had the means to travel to other parts of the country so organized bus trips were common. Many works, social clubs and pubs ran these, usually on a Sunday, often called "mystery drives" where the only people knowing the destination were the organizer and the driver. Almost always on board would be a "box player", who was very often a blind man playing an accordion so the passengers could have a sing-song. Destinations varied, the most popular were Butlins at Ayr, the Borders or Fife. On the September weekend, a local holiday, Blackpool was the favourite to go and see the illuminations. People wishing to go on the trips saved a few shillings each week and weekly raffles were held to subsidise the cost of the day. If it was a works outing the cost would be subsidised by the firm.

Many of the large employers had a social club where darts and snooker tournaments were held.

At the weekends the clubs would be full with visitors having to be signed in by a member.

There was always a bingo session followed by a cabaret act often featuring big names from the entertainment world. This would be followed by dancing. Many of the clubs had a football team with varying degrees of success.

Tenement life could be difficult by today's standards but was accepted as the norm as nobody knew anything different. Large families often three generations lived in a one or two bedroom flat often with no hot water and a shared outside toilet. The only bathing facilities for some was the local council run swimming pool known as "the baths". There you could hire a cubicle with a bath for a set time. Most men did this on a Friday night after a week's work. The children would go two or three times a week getting a hot shower and a swim followed by a "shivery bite". This could be a slice of bread with jam or if you had the money a bag of chips on the way home. With little or no washing facilities in the houses some women had to take the weeks washing in a zinc bath on an old pram frame to the local wash house known as the steamie.

One enterprising man spotted an opportunity to start a business. He purchased six twin tub washing machines and with a van he delivered them to customers houses. The women could choose which day with a morning, afternoon or evening slot. It was not just washing machines that you could rent. In the early days of television most people rented their television sets.

By today's standards it is inconceivable the grip the church had on peoples lives. Sunday was sacrosanct. No shops were open, no pubs, restaurants, or places of entertainment. Even in play parks, the parkie tied up the swings and roundabouts, as children were not allowed to play outside. The only form of recreation allowed was going for a walk dressed in your Sunday best. There was nothing so dreary as a Scottish Sabbath.

In a number of streets in an area was a road sign stating CHILDRENS PLAYGROUND NO VEHICLES 4pm TILL SUNSET. This gave the local kids somewhere to play football, rounders or marbles (bools) and the girls skipping ropes or "peevers" (hopscotch).This was often under the watchful eye of an old woman or man looking out their window or as it was known "having a hing". Houses were smaller and families were larger with extended families living in close proximity to each other. Everybody knew their neighbours, and the doors were seldom locked. Maybe one of the reasons was that nobody had anything to steal. Kids often ran messages for elderly residents who were unable to go to the local shop.

Most children had a job either delivering morning papers, morning rolls or milk for one of the big dairy companies. St. Cuthberts was known locally as "the store". Edinburgh and Dumfriesshire Dairy was also known locally as the "Dummy", and Murchies Dairy. The rounds would be completed before school. Some children preferred delivering evening papers for local newsagents when they came out of school. The official age for employment was 13 and the child could not start work before 7am but this was never strictly adhered to. This gave children the work ethic and taught them how to handle money and a sense of responsibility.

There were many innocent games played in the streets by boys and girls that cost nothing except imagination. Boys played cops and robbers or cowboys and Indians which were influenced by films. By today's standards these were not politically correct as the Indians were always the baddies.

Football cards could be found in cigarette packets depicting the stars of the day. Boys would collect them and swap doublers for any that they were missing. Girls would collect scraps and change them in much the same way. With no health and safety concerns kids made swings from trees using a length of rope and an old car tyre. Another favourite was a guider or bogey made from a set of pram wheels, some scrap wood, and a length of rope for steering, no brakes, just hold your shoe against the wheel. Great favourites for the boys were football, marbles (bools), rounders were played by both boys and girls but the girls were more inclined to play with dolls, dressing up, skipping with a length of rope and using a whip and peerie. The new crazes from America were the yo-yo and hula hoop. Yo-yo competitions were held in local clubs and cinemas to promote sales. The hula hoop was invented in 1958 and 25 million were sold in four months. It was seen as a punishment for children to be kept in and not allowed out to play. The common accepted time to go home was when the street lights went on.

One of the most popular summer treats was to be taken to Portobello Open Air Pool which was opened in 1936 in the Art Deco style.

It was the biggest pool in Europe with seating for six thousand, a ten metre high diving platform and a wave machine that operated every hour. In the 1950's Sean Connery was employed as a life guard. The pool was heated by waste steam from the neighbouring power station. When the power station closed in 1978, what little heat it provided was lost, signaling the end. The pool closed in 1979 but was not demolished until 1988 to be replaced with five a side football pitches.

One form of entertainment for the children was the Band of Hope, a temperance movement whose aim was to stop children from falling under the influence of alcohol. This was done by "signing the pledge" which was a promise to abstain from consuming alcohol. Most children only went for the magic lantern show and only found out much later the true purpose. Some people even thought that the name described a man called Hope with disfigured legs (Bandy).

Long before Irving Welsh used the expression as the title of his novel and film, Trainspotting was a popular pastime for boys, and even grown men during the 1950's-60's. They would stand on railway station platforms armed with a packed lunch, pencil, and Ian Allan's book. The book listed the name, number, class and to which locomotive depot they were assigned. All 22,000 British Railways steam engines were listed. When a loco was spotted its number would be scored out in the book and boys would spend the entire day collecting numbers.

Up to the advent of television in the 1950's the only forms of entertainment in the home were the wireless or a wind up gramophone. Some of the programmes on the B.B.C. radio were Housewife's Choice and Workers Playtime. On a Sunday lunchtime an announcement, "The time in

Britain is 12 noon, in Germany its 1 o'clock but home or away its time for Two Way Family Favourites". The show was hosted by Cliff Michelmore in Cologne and Jean Metcalfe in London in conjunction with the British Forces Broadcasting Service. This was a request program keeping families in touch with loved ones serving in West Germany, but under B.B.C. strict broadcasting rules girlfriends were not allowed to be mentioned, despite a no flirting on air rule the two presenters would go on to marry. This was followed by the Billy Cotton Band show which opened with the cry "Wakey Wakey". His son would go on to be head of the B.B.C. By anybody's standards today the most bizarre was a ventriloquist on the radio. This was Educating Archie, the show hosted by Peter Brough, a ventriloquist and his dummy Archie Andrews, a naughty schoolboy. The show would provide a starting point for many future big name stars including a 14 year old Julie Andrews. The show had a regular 15 million audience and Archie's fan club would exceed 250,000. When the show transferred to T.V. it proved to be a failure as Archie had a scary look and Peter was not that good a ventriloquist. When he asked Dora Bryan if she could see his lips move she replied "only when Archie speaks". He had a royal following hosting the Christmas party at Windsor Castle for 25 years. When Brough died in 1999 the puppet was sold for a staggering £34,000.

Children had their own request program on a Saturday morning hosted by Uncle Mac (Derek McCulloch) he only played songs the B.B.C. deemed suitable for children for example "Nellie the Elephant", "The Runaway Train" "The Laughing Policeman" etc. In total about twenty songs which were repeated week after week.

Circus comes to Town

The three biggest names in traveling circuses were Bertram Mills, Billy Smarts and Chipperfields who were the biggest.

Each year their arrival was eagerly anticipated and when Bertram Mills circus arrived by train at Waverley Station they would parade along Princes Street making their way to Murrayfield where the show would be staged.

The parade was a spectacle that attracted hundreds of onlookers. In the parade there were elephants, camels, horses, clowns and jugglers who entertained the crowd and advertised the show. The peak years of the circus were 1950's and 60's. The show was held in a tent called the big top that could seat 6000 and was always a sell out.

The Chipperfield family had been involved in shows with performing animals for over 300 years, The number of animals taking part were 200 horses 16 elephants and over 200 other animals. Also part of the show were trapeze artists, jugglers and clowns all controlled by a ring master who always wore a red tail coat and a top hat.

The human performers were all world class with many coming from the continent and were stars in their own right.

As audiences declined the family started up safari parks and continued to train animals used mainly for film work.

At the peak of their popularity Corgi toys produced a range of Chipperfield circus vehicles much sought after by small boys.

As attitudes toward performing animals changed the District council placed a ban on this type of entertainment that effectively killed off this type of circus.

As people grew older their interests changed. Many turned to ballroom dancing which was a popular pastime with a plethora of good dance halls, all with a live bands. In Leith there was the Eldorado while others were Stewarts at Abbeyhill, Cavendish at Tollcross, Plaza at Morningside, Locarno on Slateford Road. The most frequented of all the Palais de Dance known locally as the "pally" on Fountainbridge where a lot of people met their future partners. There was a revolving stage that meant two orchestras could change over in the middle of a tune with no interruption to the dancing. A strict no alcohol policy was in place with only soft drinks available in "Cupids Corner". One of the doormen was a local boy named Tommy (later Sean) Connery. As a dance hall it closed in 1967 becoming a bingo hall now demolished for student accommodation.

Chapter 11

Prior to the building of housing estates in the suburbs most citizens lived in tenements in the city centre and worked locally. There was no need to travel very far as everything was on your doorstep. There were local schools and numerous shops offering a wide and diverse range of goods.

St. Cuthberts Cooperative Association known commonly as "The Store" was the biggest. Providing everything from the cradle to the grave. It was started in 1859 and had branches in every area. Customers could become members and they were given their own five or six digit number. Each purchase was recorded and at the end of each financial year they were paid a dividend or "divi" as it was known, based on the total spend. This was a welcome payment enabling parents to purchase outfits for children going back to school after the holidays. Today many of the older generation can still remember their mothers store number.

A common sight on the streets was the horse drawn milk carts making early morning deliveries of milk to their customers. They would purchase tokens from the Store which they would leave in empty milk bottles indicating how many pints they required that day. The store dairy was on Morrison Street and the stables for the horses was on Grove Street. Of the many people employed delivering milk one local boy "Big Tam" (later Sean) Connery would go on to international fame as a film star. The last horse drawn milk delivery was in 1985 after 125 years of operation. With the introduction of supermarkets shopping patterns changed and the Store went into decline. After restructuring and amalgamations it operates today as Scotmid.

One of the most recognizable shops was the Buttercup Dairy. This was due to the ceramic tiles at the entrance depicting a young girl holding a buttercup flower under the chin of a dairy cow

The business was started by Andrew Ewing with headquarters in Elbe Street and as the business expanded he moved headquarters to Easter Road in 1915. At their peak Buttercup had 250 shops employing hundreds of women. The shops had a high quality if limited range of goods, eggs, butter, margarine and condensed milk. The stores were nearly always staffed by women.

At Clermiston he established a poultry farm housing 200,000 hens occupying 86 acres which was nicknamed "hen city" again the staff were predominately female.

Andrew Ewing was a very devout Christian man who gave away to hospitals and charities all eggs laid on a Sunday. This amounted to over 5 million a year.

The depression of the 1930's saw the company struggle due in part to his generous donations to charity and a devastating fire at the poultry farm in 1936. This effectively saw the end of that part of his business and led to large scale closure of shops over the following years and by the 1950's only 30 remained. The last one closed in 1965. There are still some shops where the ceramic tiles have been retained to this day.

With no refrigerators housewives tended to shop on a daily basis and knew all the shopkeepers by name.

Although today the midday meal is known as lunch it used to be referred to as dinner and your evening meal was your tea.

Each year a number of men known as "Ingin Johnnys" would appear in the city. These were Breton farmers who came to sell their crop of pink onions. They were a colourful group dressed in striped jerseys and wearing berets. Hanging from the handlebars of their pushbikes they would have strings of onions which they would sell door to door all over the city and further afield. As the road and railway infrastructure to Paris was so poor the farmers found it easier to transport their produce by sea to Britain. At their peak their numbers reached fourteen hundred selling 10,000 tons of their produce. By the 1970's their numbers had diminished to 160 selling 1,100 tons. The story of them transporting their wares inspired Brittany farmers to start up Brittany ferries.

A regular feature at street corners were the fishwife's. These were a group of hardy women hailing from the fishing ports along the river Forth. Dressed in their traditional outfits, they each had their regular pitch selling their husbands catch of haddock, herring, mussels and buckies. They carried their wares in a creel on their back supported by a strap round their forehead. The load that they carried would often weigh over ½ cwt.(around 45 kilos).

One group of immigrants who added flavour to city life were the Italians. These friendly hard working people opened up ice cream shops, cafés and fish and chip shops. They never set up in the same area to avoid opposition to each other. Through hard work and long hours they came to dominate what today is known as take-away food.

With marriages between the families they were seen to be a close knit community. When Italy entered W.W.2 this community was treated harshly by the British government interring the males in case they were spies. When asked what he proposed to do with German and Italian residents Winston Churchill famously stated "collar the lot" ignoring the fact that many had come to Britain to escape the regime back home. Donaldsons school on West Coates was used as an internment camp.

Football

Chapter 12

Football often called Scotland's national game was once played on the street with a pile of jerseys for goal posts. The owner of the ball would be the captain who would pick his team. All the boys in the street would meet and the two captains would take alternate picks using what was known as "cock" or a "hen". There was no limit to the size of the team and everybody got a game that would last until the ball owner would have to go home. Many of Scotland's top professionals started this way often referred to as "tanner ba' players. They developed their skills at dribbling and ball control using anything available often a tennis ball.

Boys would graduate from street football to organized games with the school, Boy Scouts, Boys Brigade or local youth club before playing for one of the many amateur teams playing in the city.

Most of the large employers had a works team playing in one of three leagues, Tuesday, Wednesday or Saturday. Some of these teams I/e railways (three teams), Edinburgh & Dumfriesshire dairy and printing firms are all gone. One works team Ferranti Thistle became Meadowbank Thistle, due to S.F.A. rules banning works names. They later moved to Livingston and took that name. They have had some ups and downs the highlight of which has to be beating Hibernian 2-1 in 2004 League cup final.

Edinburgh City, a semi-professional club founded in 1928 played until its demise in1955 when the local council refused to renew their lease on City Park. The club continued trading as a social club on Baxters Place. In 1986 Postal United, (founded in 1966) was given permission to use the name.

Postal United who played in a pillar box red strip changed to black and white the colours of Edinburgh City and play their games at Meadowbank. During refurbishment of Meadowbank they struck a deal with Spartans to use their city park ground.

St. Bernards started out as 3rd. Edinburgh Rifle Volunteers in 1874 as part of the territorial army. But, due to the members spending too much time on football, much to the chagrin of the people in charge of the 3rd. Edinburgh Rifles, they decided to split in 1878. As they played their games in Stockbridge they took the name St. Bernards after the well on the Water of Leith and used an image of the well as the club badge. In 1880 the club moved to the Royal Patent Gymnasium, now King George V park on Eyre Place. The peak of the clubs achievements was in 1895 when they beat Hearts in a replay semi final and went on to win the Scottish cup beating Renton 2-1 in the final at Ibrox Park before a 12,000 strong crowd. The club could not compete with the domination of the two other teams, Hearts and Hibernian. They moved to New Logie Green in 1896 where they lost 1-0 in the cup semi final to Hearts who would go on to lift the cup beating city rivals Hibernian 3-1 in a match held at New Logie Green. This was the only time a final had been held outside Glasgow. A young divinity student named Leonard Small signed for the club in 1928 and would play until 1936 before the church forced him to stop playing, known as the "Holy Goalie" he would go on to become the Moderator of the Church of Scotland in 1966. The mid 1930's was the clubs best run, in season 1935-6 playing in second division they missed promotion by 3 points scoring over 100 goals a feat they would repeat in the following two seasons. In 1938 they again reached the semi finals of the Scottish Cup losing to East Fife the eventual winners after a second replay at Tynecastle Park before a crowd of 35,264 their largest gate. In 1942 during World War Two the league was shut down. Their last match was a 2-1 defeat to East Fife. The St. Bernards Supporters Club started a boys club in 1947 but attempts to resurrect the club failed. In 1951 the Supporters Club voted to disband and any funds left were used to purchase a trophy named the St. Bernards cup to be played for by local schools. St. Bernards boys club still take part in local leagues.

Edinburgh Taxi Drivers who played under the name Ecatra were a very old and feared team.

Ecatra was formed in 1924 but records show that their predecessors were also very much football minded. Representative matches were played between Edinburgh Cab Drivers (horse) and Edinburgh Taxi Drivers(motor) in the years 1911 and 1912, and going back even further, an annual competition was inaugurated in 1896 between cab drivers from the east and west areas of the city. A Mr. Somerville presented the trophy (which became known as the Somerville Cup) and the last game in this series was held in 1912.

When the Ecatra was formed in 1924 their first bid for honours was in the Mid Week Amateur League. Five years later in season 1929-30 they finished top of the league. Shortly after this they transferred to the Tuesday Amateur league for convenience.

Football activities were suspended during the war years but in 1947 Eddie Smeaton club secretary was instrumental in getting the league restarted and it went on to comprise sixteen teams in two divisions. Winning many trophies Ecatra with their fast style of play became the team no one relished playing and in winning the league in 1952 lost only one game, when they were beaten 5-3 by Telex. Playing in sky blue tops their home ground was Leith Links where they were virtually unbeatable.

Paddy Crossan, Heart of Midlothian player who fought as one of McCraes Battalion (16th. battalion Royal Scots during the First World War), and who was said to be "the handsomest man in football" who could pass a ball but not a mirror. On retiring from the professional game he became a publican on Rose Street. It was he who suggested a match between Edinburgh and Glasgow taxi drivers and he donated the medals for the first match in 1928.

In the autumn of 1928 following two friendly games between the taxi drivers of Edinburgh and Glasgow, the editor of the "Taxi World" put forward the suggestion that an "International" football match be arranged between a picked team of Scottish taxi drivers and a similar team from among that fine body of sportsmen who comprise the London cab trade. As was anticipated, the suggestion aroused the utmost enthusiasm both North and South of the Tweed, and when the British Taximeter Company kindly offered to put up a Challenge Cup and the Beardmore Taximeter Company, with equal kindness, agreed to present two sets of specially designed medals, plans were speedily prepared for the holding of the first "International" sporting event in the history of the British Taxicab industry.

Mocatra Athletic Club founded in 1922 is the acronym for the Motor Cab Trade an organization in London promoting sport in the cab trade with sections for angling, cricket, rifle shooting, darts, golf and football.

The fixture would go on to be an annual event alternating between the two capitals and played in the country where the home international between Scotland

and England was taking place. It is ironical to note that the Scottish cabbies had a better record than their professional counterparts against the "Auld Enemy"

Manchester was chosen as the venue for the first encounter, the Directors of Manchester City F.C. having kindly offered the free use of their magnificent ground, and the services of their international goalkeeper Sam Cowan as referee. The Manchester and Salford Owners and Drivers' Association expressing pleasure at the opportunity of giving their fellow drivers from London and Edinburgh a generous sample of Lancashire hospitality. The Chief Constable of the City (Mr. J Maxwell) and Alderman Carter; Chairman of the Hackney Carriage Committee, along with other members of the City Council evinced the keenest interest in this sporting enterprise of the cab trade. Alderman Carter agreed to perform the kick off ceremony while the Chief Constable (a Scot by the way!) not only attended the match, but also the celebration dinner in the evening. In presenting the cup and the medals, he paid glowing tribute to the fine sporting spirit of taxi-drivers as a whole.

The Scottish Taxi Trade's representatives returned to Edinburgh on the morning of Thursday, April 18th. 1929, with the cup, having defeated the London *Mocatra* team 1-0.

The proceeds of this match were given to the widow of a Manchester taxi driver, who had been killed in an accident when he drove into the Manchester Ship Canal during a thick fog. Since then the proceeds of the annual match have been given to a charity and many hundreds of pounds have been raised over the years.

In the following year, 1930, the match between the two cities took place in Edinburgh; on Wednesday April 9th.on the famous Tynecastle Park ground, kindly placed at the trades disposal by the Directors of "Heart of Midlothian" F.C. and once again civic recognition was accorded the cab trade. Bailie Dickson, one of the senior Magistrates of the Scottish capital and Chairman of the Hackney Carriage

Committee. He kindly offered to kick off and afterward present the cup and medals to the contesting teams.

His tribute to the inherent sportsmanship of taxicab drivers was no less eloquent than that of the Chief Constable of Manchester, while the cab trade of Edinburgh gave their colleagues from London abundant proof that a Scot is second-to-none when it comes to dispensing hospitality.

As to football skill, there was little to choose between the English side and the Scots, but the latter retained possession of the cup by a 2-1 victory over the *"Mocatra"* eleven. The medals that year were presented by Messrs. W. Watson & Co. (Liverpool) Ltd., the distributors of the Morris-Commercial taxicab.

One of the attractions at these games were the officials. In 1949 the linesmen were Tommy Walker (Hearts and Scotland) and Eddie Turnbull (Hibs and Scotland) the game being played at Easter Road with Scotland winning 1-0. In 1950 the linesmen were Tommy Walker (Hearts) Gordon Smith (Hibs and Scotland) at Easter Road with Scotland winning 3-0. 1952 again at Easter Road the linesmen Willie Bauld (Hearts and Scotland) Willie Ormond (Hibs and Scotland) Scotland won 2-1.

The 25th. Meeting between the clubs took place again at Easter Road Stadium in 1954 and the linesmen on the day were Willie Bauld (Hearts) and Willie Woodburn (Rangers and Scotland) the Scots would be 3-2 winners taking their total wins to 11 with England 6.

In 1956 at Easter Road linesmen on the day were Bobby Parker (Hearts and Scotland) Willie Ormond (Hibs) with England 2-1 winners.

1965 the game was played in London, with Bobby Robson (Fulham and England) the referee, Scotland won 2-1.

Ecatra would go on to compete in league and cup competitions until their demise in the 1990's.

The professional game in the city is contested by two clubs Hearts from Gorgie and Hibs from Easter Road and depending where you were brought up was where your loyalties would lie. Hibs support mainly coming from Leith and Hearts from the west of the city. In those days it was allowed for alcohol to be consumed at matches, it was also common practice for small boys to stand at the turnstile and ask men to lift them over thus avoiding the entrance fee. The operator of the turnstile would turn a blind eye and once in the ground and the boys would search for empty beer bottles on which there was a deposit payable on their return to the pub where they were sold. Carrying sacks, hordes of boys would clear the terracing after the match and then head to the nearest pub to cash in.

Hibernian Football Club was founded in 1875 by a group of Irish immigrants who lived in the Cowgate and attended St. Patricks church. It was named from the Roman name for Ireland, Hibernia. The club badge has three emblems the Irish harp representing its Irish roots, a castle representing Edinburgh and a galleon which is on Leith's coat of arms. The harp was dropped from the badge in the 1950's and reintroduced when the badge was redesigned in 2000.The colour of the jerseys is green and white and has been since the formation of the club. Hibs were the first team, in 1977 to have sponsors names on their shirts a move that made television companies threaten to boycott their games unless they wore an alternative strip.

Due to mismanagement in 1891 the club ceased playing but soon reformed. One of the changes introduced at that time was that it was no longer a requirement for young men to belong to the Catholic Young Men's Society.

In 1887 when a young priest in Glasgow started a football club to raise money to feed the poor he copied the formula used by Hibernian and the team was named Celtic. The new club then signed up a large number of Hibernian players who would go on to be the catalyst for Celtic teams of the future.

They first won the league in 1903 again in 1948 and they had back to back wins in 1952 and 1953. Their record in the Scottish Cup however is not impressive. They won it in 1887 and 1902 and were runners up eleven times including back to back finals in 2012 and 2013. The 2012 defeat was probably the hardest on the support as a 5-1 thrashing by local rivals Heart of Midlothian gave the Gorgie side of the city bragging rights. However the support had plenty to cheer about when they finally lifted the trophy in 2016.

The most successful period in the clubs history was in the post war era of the late 1940's and early 1950's.

This was the era of the "Famous Five" the forward line of Gordon Smith, Bobby Johnstone, Lawrie Reilly, Eddie Turnball and Willie Ormand and is regarded as the finest seen in Scottish football. They played together from 1949 until 1955 when Johnstone was sold to Manchester City. Each player scored over one hundred goals and were unfortunate not to win more honours.

Hibs were the first British team to take part in a European tie. In 1955 eighteen clubs who were thought to be a big draw and had floodlit grounds were invited to take part in what would become the European Cup, forerunner of the Champions League. English club Chelsea were persuaded by Football League secretary Alan Hardacre not to participate. Hibs reached the semi-final but were beaten 3-0 on aggregate by Stade Reims who in turn would be beaten by Real Madrid at the start of their extraordinary run of wins.

Eddie Turnball returned to Easter Road as manager in 1971 and created what would be known as "Turnball's Tornadoes" who played scintillating football winning the league cup in 1972 finishing runners up in the league in 1974 and 1975 winning the Drybrough cup in 1972 and 73 but giving most pleasure to their support was the 7-0 hammering of local rivals Hearts in the New Year's day derby 1973. Turnball resigned in 1980 and the club went into a decline resulting in relegation in 1980. They were promoted the following season but failed to challenge for honours. This would prove to be the blackest time in the clubs history.

Towards the end of Turnball's tenure Chairman Tom Hart signed George Best on what was reported to be £2,000 a week, it was a move that did more for gate receipts than results as Best was a shadow of his former self due to his alcoholic addiction. He would play only twenty two times.

Due to mismanagement in the 1980's when Duff and Gray were at the helm Hibs were on the brink of financial ruin. In 1990 Wallace Mercer chairman of Hearts attempted a hostile takeover. He said it would be a merger but fans saw it as the end of the club and formed the fighting group Hand of Hibs which included celebrity fans such as the Proclaimers, Irving Welsh and Marillion front man Fish, even Hearts fans joined in to save the club and Kwik Fit owner Sir Tom Farmer was persuaded to step in with a financial package when it was discovered that a relative of his had helped save the club in 1891. Following the attempted takeover Hibs had a few good years in the early 1990's winning the League cup in 1991 and recording three top five finishes in the League. The following years were not kind to Hibs. They had to sell their best players to stay afloat, hovering from the middle of the table into the bottom half before being relegated.

The stadium has been completely remodeled since 1995 with the north stand being named the Famous Five stand and the famous "Easter Road slope" on the pitch was leveled out.

Their record is not as good as it should have been despite long periods with talented players playing scintillating football but trophies were destined to go elsewhere. They have won the League Championship four times (1902-3, 1947-48, 1950-51,1951-52) and been runners up six times (1897-96, 1946-7, 1949-50, 1952-53, 1973-74, 1974-75) Scottish cup winners three times (1886-87,1901-02, 2015-16) and runners up eleven times(1895-

96,1913-14, 1922-23,1946-47, 1957-58,1971-72,1978-79,2000-01, 2011-12, 2012-13) League Cup winners three times (1972-73,1991-92,2006-07) and runners up seven times(1950-51,1968-69,1974-75,1985-86, 1993-94, 2003-04 2015-16) second division champions six times (1893-94,1894-95,1932-33,1980-81,1998-99,2016-17)

Drybrough Cup winners in 1972 and 1973 Since 2000 the revolving door was fitted to the managers office with eleven holding the position up to 2018. In 2014 Leanne Dempster was appointed chief executive a job mirrored at Tynecastle with Ann Budge in charge.

On the west side of town the loyalties predominately lie with Heart of Midlothian F.C. known in rhyming slang as Jam tarts or Jambos for short. The club was founded in 1874 by a group of youths who frequented a dance hall of that name. They played their early games at the Meadows, Powburn and Logie Green before moving to old Tynecastle in 1881 now the site of Wardlaw Place and Terrace. They played their early games in red and blue jerseys but during the wash the colours ran and from then on it has been maroon. The club crest is based on a mosaic on the High Street at the site of the former Tolbooth prison immortalized in Sir Walter Scotts novel The Heart of Midlothian. The first captain was Tom Purdie grandson of Sir Walters friend and gamekeeper Tom Purdie.

In 1886 they played their first match at new Tynecastle beating Bolton 4-1 the scorer of the first goal at Tynecastle was Tommy Jenkinson. The Scottish League was formed in in 1890 with Hearts as one of the founder members.

1891 saw Hearts lift the Scottish cup for the first time when they beat Dumbarton at Hampden a feat they would repeat a further seven times in 1896, 1901, 1906, 1956, 1998, 2005 and 2012 and being runner up seven times. The most satisfying wins for the Gorgie boys must be beating their local rivals Hibs in two finals, The first in 1896 was held at New Logie Green the only time a final has been held outside Glasgow and in 2012 thrashing them 5-1. When they won in 1956 they only conceded one goal in the competition and that was against Celtic in the final. 334,000 watched their six games in the competition. 133,000 people were at the final the largest crowd to watch a Hearts game.

During the game "Iron Man" John Cummings split open his forehead in a clash with Celtics Willie Fernie. No substitutes were allowed at the time so Cumming, with blood streaming down his face was taken to the touch line where stitches were inserted. With his head bandaged he returned to the field after issuing the words "blood does not show on a maroon jersey" That quote is now displayed above the entrance to the players tunnel at Tynecastle. He was awarded Man of the Match.

In season 1894-95 the club won the league championship for the first time and would do so again in 1897, 1958 1960 and they were runners up fourteen times. In the Scottish League Cup they have not proved so successful winning in 1954 1958 1959 1962 and runners up in 1961 1996 2013.

1932 saw the arrival of Tommy Walker aged seventeen who would go on to become a club legend. He was transferred to Chelsea in 1947 for £6,000 and at the end of his playing career returned to Tynecastle in 1951 as manager were he would remain for sixteen years winning seven trophies and never out of the top four in the league. He would oversee a golden period in the clubs history and under his regime Hearts never had a player red carded. Davie MacLean became manager in 1941 and his signings would be the foundation of a great team sadly he died before it came to fruition. October 1948 saw the "Terrible Trio" consisting of Alfie Conn, Willie Bauld and Jimmy Wardhaugh play together for the first time they would go on to score an incredible 950 goals between them before splitting up in 1958.The 1959 League Cup final was won with a 2-1 victory over Third Lanark. Jocky Robertson Thirds goalie and an avid Hearts fan wore a Hearts jersey under his goalkeeper jersey the only time a player has worn the opposing teams colours in a major final.

Season 1964-5 was complete disaster for the Gorgie support. At that time the league was decided on goal average not on the present day goal difference Hearts were two points clear with one game to go a home match at Tynecastle against Willie Waddell's Kilmarnock who were in second place and required to win by two goals. These were scored in the first half, Hearts were unable to respond. The final score was Hearts 0 Kilmarnock 2 and the league title went to Rugby Park by 0.4 of a goal, the closest difference in Scottish football history.

Subsequently, Hearts were instrumental in pushing through a change to use goal difference to separate teams level on points. Ironically this rule change later denied Hearts the title in 1985–86.

Many of the support believe that this was the start of a bleak time in the clubs history that would last twenty years. The depths of despair were felt when on New Years day 1973 during the new years derby they were comprehensively thrashed 7-0 by local rivals Hibs a team known quite rightly as Turnbulls Tornadoes.

The Gorgie boys had nothing to celebrate in 1977 when the team was relegated for the first time in their history. This began a sequence of yo-yoing between the Premier League and First Division six times in seven seasons finally gaining promotion to the premier league in 1983.

A 6-2 defeat by St. Mirren after leading 1-0 in August 1985 began the start of the "Mita Season" when they might have won the league and might have won the cup. Ironically jersey sponsors were Mita and Hearts had an unbeaten 31 game -27 in the league run, losing the last game in a 2-0 away defeat to Dundee. With just seven minutes to go substitute Albert Kidd scored and three minutes later scored again, this combined with Celtic winning 5–0 against St Mirren meant the top two clubs finished the season on the same number of points. Hearts lost out to Celtic by a goal difference of three. Had goal difference been the rule in 1965 Hearts would have been champions; had goal average still applied in 1986, they would have won the league. Hearts lobbying after the league loss in 1965 cost them dear in 1986.

The following Saturday a demoralized team were beaten by Alex Ferguson's Aberdeen 3-0 in the cup final.

When Tommy Walker retired in 1966 the club installed a revolving door to the managers office with occupants lasting only a maximum five years. In total there have been 28 up to 2017 out of a total number for the club since its inception of 37. This led to disappointing results and the inevitable financial crisis. Things came to a head in 2004 when chairman Chris Robinson announced that Tynecastle stadium would have to be sold to pay club debts and entered into a deal with Cala Homes. Later that year Vladimir Romanov entered talks to buy the club, clear the debts and promised the club would remain at Tynecastle. The support got behind him and he bought out Robinson. By 2005 he was in complete control and under his stewardship the club debt was transferred from H.B.O.S to Ukio Bankas a financial institution controlled by Romanov. By 2007 the debt had spiraled to £36 million and on several occasions players wages were late in being paid and the club was threatened with administration twice. The 2005 season got of to a flying start with George Burley as manager Hearts won their first eight league matches and were top of the league when Romanov stunned the support by sacking Burley. He promised a top class replacement but that never materialized and he went from hero to villain when in 2012 Hearts were handed a winding up order by the court over failure to pay a tax bill. 2013 saw the club enter administration and they were docked a third of the previous seasons points tally meaning they would start the season minus fifteen points and would be relegated in 2014. The support rallied round and bought season tickets taking the total to over 10,000 giving the club a chance of survival. A deadline of 2013 for interested parties to put in formal bids for the club which was won by supporters group The Foundation of Hearts. In 2014 Ann Budge took control and with the financial help of the support the club exited administration in 2014 thus ending Vlad the Mad's involvement with the club. With a new stadium and financial stability the future looks promising for the Gorgie Boys.

McCraes Battalion

And

Heart of Midlothian Football Club

Chapter 13

In Edinburgh at the Haymarket intersection stands the Hearts clock, a memorial unique in this country.

It commemorates the members of Heart of Midlothian football club who gave their lives for their country in the two world wars but was erected to honour the players who were killed or died of their wounds in the first world war and was paid for by the supporters of the club.

In today's world of professional football where players of mediocre talent can command huge salaries and behave like spoiled children it is inconceivable the sacrifice these men made when they were top of the league and were by far the best team in Scotland.

During 1914 as reports came back from France about the backs to the wall fighting and the number of casualties grew, campaigns were launched to improve recruitment figures. Most famous of these was the Lord Kitchener poster depicting him pointing and the slogan "YOUR COUNTRY NEEDS YOU". Other jingoistic orators including Lord Durham who exhorted young men to volunteer to join him in fighting "The Hun" although he himself had no intention of going of to France albeit he was too old. He condemned the number of people going to football matches to watch professionals playing football when they should be in the trenches being slaughtered, ignoring the fact that many on the terracing were already in uniform or were exempt on the grounds of being too old or too young. Many were in reserved occupations, either medically unfit or the sole wage earners for a family. It seems strange that football was singled out for such criticisms.

In one incident, misguided and ill informed young ladies (and I use the word advisedly) handed out white feathers, the symbol of cowardice, to some Hearts players and this had a profound effect in the dressing room.

One local prominent businessman Sir George McCrae approached the war office for permission to raise a battalion on condition that he would lead it into battle. When permission was granted he stated that he would raise it in one week. He contacted the Hearts board and they gave him permission to approach the players. At a meeting in the boardroom eleven players joined up with five others being rejected on medical grounds. A total of 75 football clubs professional and amateur contributed players with other sportsmen volunteering for what would become known as "McCraes Battalion".

McCrae set up a recruiting office in Castle Street and held a recruiting rally in the Usher Hall with the Hearts players on the platform. When he announced to a packed hall that he was going to sign up and that anyone who wished could follow him to the recruiting office. The hall emptied and young men fought to get into the recruiting office.

True to his word, McCrae raised the Battalion, 1320 men in a week and the war office named it 16th. Battalion Royal Scots, although the men called it "McCraes" after their charismatic colonel as he was their leader and it was for him that they had signed up, When billeted in George Heriots School and with no uniforms available due to the shortage of khaki material word arrived that there were four wagons of material in a nearby railway siding, which were bound for England. McCrae and some of his men went on night exercises armed with crowbars. Using Territorial Army patterns and some local penal institutions the Battalion had their uniforms in a week.

McCrae told his men that they would be the yardsticks that the rest of Kitcheners Army would be judged against.

It is interesting to note that before mobilization during the period August to December Hearts league position was

Played	Won	Lost	Drawn	Goals Scored	Goals Conceded	Points
21	19	1	1	52	13	39

After mobilization, January to April

Played	Won	Lost	Drawn	Goals Scored	Goals Conceded	Points
17	8	3	6	31	20	22

Army training is not the best training for footballers and it showed in Hearts performances, indeed on occasions they returned from night route marches in time to catch the train for away games. In a close finish Celtic Football Cub pipped them for the League Title with Glasgow Rangers 11 points further back. It is interesting to note that neither of the two Glasgow clubs had players who would join the colours.

On arrival in France, ironically on the Kaiser's birthday McCraes were almost constantly in the front line at the Somme and the Battalion was almost wiped out at Contalmaison. 800 made the supreme sacrifice. Of the Hearts players 7 were killed, three on the first day of the Somme offensive. None of their bodies were ever recovered and McCrae himself was invalided home due to his wounds. He died in 1928, his death being attributed to his war wounds.

It is estimated that 100,000 people dressed in black lined the route of the funeral cortege from Lady Glenorchy's church in Roxburgh Place to Grange cemetery a distance of 3 miles. As one surviving member of the battalion recalled "it was eerie, total silence, not even a cough, only the sound of horses hoofs and the trundle of wheels over the cobbles. At a reunion dinner in 1919 it was agreed that a memorial should be erected at Contalmaison. This was finally achieved in 2005 thanks largely due to Jack Alexander author of the outstanding book "McCraes Battalion" and Tom Purdie grandson of the first Hearts captain and ex Cab Inspector in Edinburgh.

Each year a group of local children and supporters of the club make a pilgrimage to the memorial on the 1st. July the date of the opening battle of the Somme.

Each year on Remembrance Sunday a service is held at the memorial known to everyone as the "Hearts Clock" attended by club officials, players and supporters. During 2006 season the Scottish Football Association (SFA) incurred the wrath of supporters when they would not allow a change of kick off time (2pm) at the away match with Aberdeen to allow the players to attend the service.

Ice Skating, Boxing

Chapter 14

In the 1950's a popular way to meet members of the opposite sex was ice skating, there were two rinks. Haymarket ice rink which opened in 1912 on Haymarket Terrace and was home to curling and recreational skating until closure in 1978 when the curling club moved to Murrayfield ice rink which was built in 1938 and is the largest permanently seated indoor arena in Scotland with a capacity of 3,800. Its opening co-coincided with the outbreak of war and the building was requisitioned for the duration.

It opened as an ice rink in 1952 with events from professional ice hockey to professional ice shows and on Friday and Saturday nights there would be up to 1,000 skaters on the rink.

Amateur boxing tournaments were also held there. The arena was a venue for the boxing events during the 1970 Commonwealth Games.

Murrayfield Royals was the name of the ice hockey team from 1952-8 when it changed to Edinburgh Royals until 1966 when Royals disappeared from the British Ice Hockey scene.

Murrayfield Racers began in 1966 until 1994 when it had a name change to become Edinburgh Racers. It would only last a year before becoming Murrayfield Royals for one season before becoming Edinburgh Capitals.

As the Racers they won the British Championship four times and in 1986/7 and 87/88 won the British Hockey League Championship.

Harlem Globetrotters the legendary American Basketball team have played the venue three times to sell-out crowds.

Amateur boxing in Edinburgh has a long and distinguished history and today clubs are still going strong, providing exercise and discipline to young boys and also to young girls thanks to the film Million Dollar Baby and double Olympic and World champion Nicola Adams.

Many people north and south of the border believe Glasgow to be the first city of fisticuffs but that is a myth and cannot be squared with historical facts.

Benny Lynch from Glasgow was regarded by many to be the first Scot to win a World title in boxing, but that is not the case. The first World Champion was a modest young man named Johnny Hill, born in a tenement at 5 Brunswick Road in 1905. Coached by his father, a former boxer and "Tancy" Lee of Leith Victoria boxing club he became the Scottish Flyweight and Bantamweight Champion. Turning professional he captured the British, European and World titles in an astonishing eighteen-month period. Whilst training he caught a chill and died of Pneumonia aged twenty-three in 1928.

Hugh Rodden from Musselburgh who took the bronze medal in the 1908 Olympics in London was the first Scotsman to win an Olympic medal. He later turned professional and emigrated to New York where he won a record twenty-three fights in a row. His gloves owned by boxing correspondent Brian Donald are on permanent display in the Royal Museum of Scotland on Chambers Street.

Big time Professional boxing was brought to Scotland by Nat Dresner a Jewish pawnbroker from Leith. He arranged matches at various venues, including Forrest Road Drill Hall and Waverley Market (now Princes Mall) often thousands being turned away because the venue was full. When he arranged a card that included Ted "Kid" Lewis v. Tommy Milligan at the Industrial Hall on Annandale Street (now Lothian bus garage) twenty thousand people crammed into the Hall, but due to the late running of three special trains from Glasgow many of

Milligan's supporters could not gain entry so they charged the turnstiles. The police responded with a baton charge to restore order. Two thousand people in the Hall had their admission charge 2s 10d (14pence) returned because they could not see. This was also the first time in Scotland that a boxing match was filmed for exhibition in cinemas. It's ironical that Nat Dressner should die on the morning of Saturday 31st. March 1928 the day that the "Wembley Wizards" beat England 5-1 at Wembley Stadium.

The end of one legend, the start of another.

Leith Victoria A A C was founded in 1919 by Dockers working in Victoria Dock to give them somewhere to train during their lunch break. It is now based in the Bell Gymnasium (named after the Bell family) in Academy Street.

One of the most illustrious boxers from the club was James "Tancy" Lee (Featherweight) the first Scot to win a Lonsdale Belt outright. He beat the legendary Welshman Jimmy Wilde ("the Ghost with a hammer in his glove"). One of his other opponents was J Matthews the "Fighting barber of Hanley" and father to the great footballer Stanley. His two nephews George and John McKenzie were both boxers and were the first brothers to win a medal at the Olympics, George a Bronze at the 1920 games in Antwerp, James a Silver at the 1924 games in Paris. They would all meet with tragic deaths in 1941.

"Tancy" died after being knocked down by a bus in Gloucester Place during a blackout in the Second World War. George committed suicide by drinking Lysol in his house on Great Junction Street and James committed suicide in a public toilet in Baileyfield Road.

Bill Sutherley (Heavyweight) entered the Guinness book of records when aged 18years 11days he became the youngest boxer to win a national title. Tragically he lost both legs when involved in an accident on a North Sea oil rig.

Alex (Happy) Howden (Light Middleweight) was a bus driver and good boxer who after retiring was still flooring people but then with laughter after becoming a stand up comic and a good supporter of many charities. He turned to acting and played the part of the hangman in the film Gangs of New York.

Willie Black Scottish Bantamweight Champion who during an International with Morocco, held in 1969 in Govan Town Hall in a moment of frustration with the Moroccan referee lashed out and floored the official and was banned sine die.

Jackie Brown (Flyweight) was the 1958 Commonwealth Gold Medalist who suffered only eight defeats in a 145-bout career. During a six-year professional career he beat or drew with three World Champions.

In 1962 he became the third former Leith Victoria boxer to win a Lonsdale Belt outright.

February 27th. 1962 was an important and eventful day in his life. In the early hours of the morning his wife gave birth to their first daughter. That evening he won the British Flyweight title against Brian Cartwright hours after walking away unscathed when the car he was traveling in was involved in a car crash during a snowstorm.

He was inducted into the boxing Hall of Fame in 2006.

On retiring from boxing he ran a box-exercise class at Marco's Leisure Centre in Grove Street and when that closed, now in his seventies he continued to run the class at Boroughmuir Rugby Club. He retired and emigrated to Australia where he died in January 2020.

Committee Member and referee George Smith has had a great career. The highlight of which has to be refereeing the bout between Henry Cooper and the then Cassius Clay (Muhammad Ali) when Coopers left hook floored the future World Champion.

In 2006 Claire Ward a classroom assistant at Tynecastle High School became the first female coach at Leith Victoria.

Alex Arthur became the eighth former member of Leith Victoria to take a British title. He also won Scottish ABA titles at Flyweight, Bantamweight and Featherweight; representing Scotland fifty six times he won bronze and silver in International competitions and took Gold at the 1998 Commonwealth Games in Kuala Lumpur. Turning professional in 2000 he won the World Boxing Organization Super Featherweight title. His record is very impressive twenty-seven bouts, twenty-six wins, nineteen by knockout.

One of the most famous boxing clubs is Sparta AAC. It was founded in 1945 by former boxer Jimmy Robertson and named after the Sparta club in Copenhagen. The club which was based on MacDonald Road has produced some of the best boxers ever to grace a ring.

The premises under threat from developers since 2000 finally closed in 2006 and found a temporary home in Shrub Place before finding what is hoped to be permanent premises in a former church opposite Meadowbank Stadium.

A story is told that one night the door opened and a young lad wearing a school blazer walked in and asked coach George Shaw "How long does it take to become a champion?". If Shaw had known of his determination he would surely have replied "Its only a matter of time". The young lads name was Bobby Neil and he would go on to become a champion despite several setbacks outside the ring. He injured his knee playing rugby, broke his wrist doing the high jump, had two bouts of rheumatic fever and shortly before his eighteenth birthday was hit by a motor cycle that shattered his hip. Eighteen months of surgery left one leg an inch shorter than the other, but through all the pain he never lost his desire to become a champion. He won titles at every amateur level and represented Scotland at International level. He turned professional in 1955 under legendary London manager Sam Burns, winning the Scottish Featherweight title in 1956. Returning from a bout in Glasgow he survived a near fatal car crash at Newbridge on the outskirts of Edinburgh and amazingly was back in the ring within eighteen months. In one of his first comeback fights against Belgian Andre Devisch he suffered a broken jaw and continued for another eight rounds to take the decision. 1959 saw Neil take the British Featherweight title in Nottingham after flooring fellow Scot Charlie Hill no less than ten times. In the first defense of the British title against ex Olympic champion, cockney Terry Spinks, whom he had stopped the previous year. Referee Ike Powell stopped the fight for what Neil believed to be a cut of "shaving nick" proportions and he always maintained that he had been robbed of his British title. Two months later in the rematch at Wembley Arena Neil was out-boxed for thirteen rounds by Spinks before being floored by a right hook and after a count of eight was knocked out by a right cross and an uppercut. During a post match interview in his dressing room Neil collapsed and was rushed to Wembley Hospital for emergency surgery to remove a blood clot from his brain. This would end his career as a boxer and start his career as a coach, trainer and manager to such fighters as Vernon Sollas, Alan Rudkin, Johnny Pritchett and Alan Minter to British and World title status.

The most famous ex member of Sparta is Ken Buchanan who won the World title in 1970.

Brought up in the Council housing scheme of Northfield. Buchanan joined Sparta aged eight and lied about his age to get membership. After a successful amateur career he turned professional in 1965 winning twenty-three consecutive bouts and in 1968 knocked out Maurice Cullen to become British Lightweight Champion. Wearing Buchanan tartan shorts and Dressing gown and being piped into the ring to the tune of Scotland the Brave the good looking boxer was a promoters dream. A points defeat against Spaniard Miguel Velazquez in Madrid for the European title which Buchanan puts down to the local judges favouring the hometown man. In 1970 promoters gave him a shot at the World title against Ismael Laguna in

San Juan, Puerto Rico in what was to be a warm up fight for Laguna before a title fight against a promising young boxer named Roberto Duran. In incredible 120-degree heat Tommy his father and corner man had to borrow a parasol from a spectator to give him some shade between rounds. He took the title after fifteen rounds when no one including the British press gave him any chance against a talented fighter such as Laguna in his own backyard. The World Boxing Council and the British Boxing Board refused to recognize him as champion but the following year he beat Rueben Navarro in Los Angeles and this time was recognized as World Lightweight champion. On his return he paraded the championship belt from an open top bus when the streets were thronged with well-wishers. Never having a fight in his hometown was always a source of irritation to Buchanan but he did top the bill at Madison Square Gardens in New York seven times, a record for a European fighter.

He was very popular with sports writers in America and in 1970 won the American Boxing Writers Association Fighter of the Year award beating Muhammad Ali and Joe Frazier into second and third place.

His defeat against Roberto Duran of Panama in Madison Square Gardens in 1972 would have an effect on the rest of his career. After 13 rounds Buchanan was ahead on points when he was floored by a low blow landed after the bell had gone for the end of the round. The referee Tony Lobianco did not punish the foul but instead awarded the bout to Duran after deciding that Buchanan could not continue, without even asking him. It would be the only time Lobianco would referee a title fight.

Duran who would go on to be one of boxing's biggest stars would not give Buchanan a rematch as had been promised and in an interview with Boxing writer Hugh McIllvaney he stated that Buchanan was the best opponent he had ever faced in the ring.

In 1973 he regained the British Lightweight title when he defeated future World Champion Jim Watt from

Glasgow and won the Lonsdale Belt outright. He then took the European title when he defeated Italian Antonio Puddu and narrowly missed the World Boxing Council title when he narrowly lost on points to Ishimatsu Suzuki in Tokyo in 1975. He went into semi-retirement before finally retiring in 1983 on doctor's advice due to the damage done to his left eye. With a record of sixty-two wins and eight defeats most of these came at the end of his career against opponents who would never have been in the ring with him in his prime, a sad end to a great career. He is the only living British boxer to be inducted into the International Boxing Hall of Fame.

He opened a hotel on Ferry Road and was a popular Mine Host. On the wall in the bar was a large photograph of him dancing with Princess Anne the night they won BBC Sports Personality of the Year. Some people think that he never got over the way he lost the World title and he started to drink heavily. His personal life went to pieces, his wife Carol divorced him and he had to sell his hotel. He returned to his trade as a joiner. He had a couple of attempts at running a public house but that was not the best environment for someone in his condition.

Danny Flynn a member of Meadowbank club was Scottish Bantamweight Champion from fourteen until he turned professional aged seventeen under manager Tommy Gilmore. He represented Scotland many times including the World Junior Championships in Yokohama. In 1979 he fought three British Champions Dave "Boy" McCauley whom he beat at Flyweight, Robert Dickie whom he beat at Bantamweight to take the Scottish title and Duke McKenzie who took the decision at Flyweight.

He worked at Kwik Fit before opening the Union Motor Company repairing cars and taxis and can still make people grimace in pain but now it's when they get their bill.

Commonwealth gold medalist Super-Middleweight Kenny Anderson from Craigmillar Boxing Club turned professional in 2006 and won his first four bouts three by knockout.

Eddie Carson, known as Napoleon due to his facial resemblance to the French Emperor Boneparte was a member of the Melbourne Club and fought Peter Keenan from Glasgow in the Scottish Bantamweight Championship, Keenan who would become a double Lonsdale Belt winner refused to fight him again saying he made too much use of the third glove (his head) and he was the dirtiest fighter who ever stepped into a ring. A bit at odds with his upbringing as a choirboy in St. Mary's Episcopalian Cathedral on Palmerston Place. At work on a building site in 1950 his manager told him he had arranged a fight with Jackie Patterson ex World Champion, the snag was he only had two hours to prepare, he accepted the fight and knocked Patterson out in the fourth round.

Eugene Henderson became a referee by chance, a fortunate one for him as it led to a career spanning forty years and saw him the third man in numerous world title fights including "Sugar" Ray Robinson v. Randolph Turpin when Turpin took the World title.

The morning headlines of Tuesday 9th. March 1971 should have read "Gorgie boy beats Ali" sounds incredible but true. The Gorgie boy was Danny McAlinden who although being born in Ireland was brought up in 21 Wardlaw Place, he would go on to take the British Heavyweight title from Jack Bodell. Billed as "The fighting Irishman from Coventry" he got the decision in a fight with Rahman Ali, brother to "The Greatest" in Madison Square Gardens on the same bill as Muhammad Ali v. Joe Frazier for the undisputed Heavyweight Championship of the World.

Golf

Chapter 15

Today St. Andrews is regarded as the home of golf. And the Royal and Ancient Club, as golf's rule giving authority. But this was not always the case, and Edinburgh's claim has the most historical validity.

Golf was played at Leith Links during the reign of the Stewarts, and Mary Queen of Scots is said to have played there.

The world's oldest golf club is the Honourable Company of Edinburgh golfers which played for its first trophy, a silver club on the Links at Leith on 7th. March 1744.

The first Rules of Golf were written at Leith, Edinburgh in 1744. An appeal was made to the Town Council of Edinburgh for a Silver Club to be awarded annually to the winner of an 'Open Golf Competition'. The Council agreed to offer such a prize but only if rules of play were drawn up and so the first-ever recorded written rules of golf were set down and signed by John Rattray who won the competition three times.

The original rules form the basis of the Rules of Golf we know today. Rattray was a surgeon and served as Surgeon General to Bonnie Prince Charlie's forces in the 1745 uprising. He was captured at Culloden and sentenced to death for treason. Golf came to his rescue when his golfing partner Lord Duncan Forbes of Culloden secured his release.

To recognize the origins of the Rules of Golf and John Rattray's achievements Leith Rules Golf Society raised funds to erect a statue of John Rattray on Leith Links. The statue was unveiled by the current captain in September 2019.

The paper on which the original 13 rules of golf were drafted is in the archives of the Honourable Company and a copy is on show at their clubhouse at Muirfield.

The Royal and Ancient club simply adopted the Leith clubs rules and it was not until 1754 that St. Andrews played for a silver club.

It was in 1834 that the St. Andrews club successfully petitioned King William 1V to designate it Royal and Ancient.

The original course at Leith was of five holes, Thorntree 414 yards, Braehead 461yards, Sawmill 426 yards, North-mid 495 yards, South-mid 435 yards. Bearing in mind the equipment available the game was all about strength and if the five holes had been eighteen as today the course would measure over 8000 yards with a SSS of 79.

In the mid 19th century the Leith Links was becoming overcrowded with grazing animals and women drying their washing so the Honourable Company moved to Musselburgh and in 1891 moved to their present home at Muirfield.

The second and third oldest clubs are the Edinburgh Burgess Golfing Society and the Bruntsfield Links golf club, the Burgess claims to have existed since 1735 but its records only go back to 1773, Bruntsfield dates back to 1761 as a society and 1787 as a club, both started at Bruntsfield Links on a six hole course with the Golf Tavern as their clubhouse.

But again with overcrowding and the decline of the links they moved to Musselburgh before moving to their present homes at Barnton and Davidsons Mains.

A pitch and putt course is still at Bruntsfield and is part of the original links so it has a claim to be the oldest course on which golf is still played.

There are 22 courses in the city boundary's, six of which are municipally owned with a number of driving ranges.

Fearing a war with England and the lack of practice at archery in 1457 James 11 laid down a statute "futeball and golfe to be utterly cryed doon and not to be used" but it appears to have had little effect and in 1503 James 1V played golf, indeed when Captain Topham visited Edinburgh he wrote "the diversion which is peculiar to Scotland, and in which all ages find great pleasure, is golf. They play at it with a small leathern ball and a piece of wood, flat on one side, in the shape of a small bat, which is fastened at the end of a stick three or four feet long, at right angles to it. The art consists of striking the ball with this instrument into a hole in the ground in a smaller number of strokes than your adversary. The game has the superiority of cricket and tennis in being less violent and dangerous, but in point of dexterity and amusement by no means to be compared with them.

Tradition says that Golfers land in the Canongate was built by John Patterson a shoemaker with the winnings of a wager.

Two English nobles challenged the Duke of York (later James V11 (11) to a game of golf and he chose Patterson as his partner. When they won, the Duke let Patterson keep the prize money which he used to build his house which was demolished in the 1950s but a plaque commemorating the feat is on the wall of the "Jenny Ha's" pub along with the family crest.

In 1798 a bet was made that no two members of the Burgess society could be found capable of driving a ball over the spire of St. Giles. A Mr Smellie, a printer and a Mr. Sceales of Leith were selected to perform this formidable task. They were allowed to use six balls each, it was reported that "the balls passed considerably higher than the weathercock and were found nearly opposite in Advocates Close".

The bet was decided early in the morning in case of accidents, the parties taking their stations at the Southeast corner of Parliament Square. The required elevation was obtained by a barrel stave, suitably fixed, and the height of the steeple, which is 161 ft. Together with the distance from the base of the church were found to be much less than a "good stroke of the club".

In 1815 a Mr. Scott betted a guinea with a Mr. McDowall that he would drive a ball from the golf house at Bruntsfield Links over Arthur's Seat in 45 strokes. Mr. Scott we learn had reason to regret his hardihood, but better luck attended a Mr. Brown who risked a gallon of whisky in a bet with a Mr Spalding that he would drive a ball over Arthur's Seat on the same terms. With his last shot Mr Brown won the whisky having cleared the lions crest in 44 strokes.

The Merchants club has a record that will never be broken in that it had two members who each won a Victoria Cross in the first and second world wars.

Baberton founded in 1893 has a clubhouse dating back to 1622 and Liberton (1920) has 18th.century Kingston Grange as its clubhouse and Ratho Parks clubhouse dates from 1824.

James Braid who was born in Elie in Fife and won the Open five times between 1901 and 1910 designed ten courses in the city.

Two of the most famous golfers the city has produced are Tommy Armour and Ronnie Shade.

Tommy Armour was brought up in Bruce Street and learned to play golf on the Braid Hills. He fought as a tank commander in the First World War in the course of which he leapt from his tank and strangled one of the enemy with his bare hands, he was gassed and wounded in the head and lost an eye. After the war he emigrated to America and became a professional golfer known as the "Silver Scot". He won the U S. open in 1927 and the U S P G A. in 1930, when the Open was first held at Carnoustie in 1931 Armour was the winner.

Ronnie Shade whose initials were R D B M. and were said to mean "right down the bloody middle" was Scotland's greatest amateur golfer, playing out of Duddingston where his father was professional, he won the Scottish Amateur Championship five times in a row from

1963-67 after being the beaten finalist in 1962. He was a Walker cup regular from 1961-1967. He won everything as an amateur and was awarded the M B E. for services to amateur golf and turned professional in 1968.

He won the Scottish professional championship as well as European tour events but he did not enjoy professional golf and he gave it up, and was reinstated as an amateur shortly before he died aged 47 in 1989.

When the European team won the Ryder Cup at Oak Hills Rochester U S A. in 1995 the P G A were presented with 100 acorns which were grown into oak trees and to mark the P G A. Centenary. They were planted at 100 golf courses through out Britain and Ireland, one of which was planted at the Braid Hills on 18th. December 2001 by Brian Donkin captain of Braids United golf club and Peter Lloyd Scottish secretary of the P G A.

In March 2003 the Leith Rules Golf Society was inaugurated. Their aim was to revive a unique piece of golfing history that belongs to Leith.

This follows on from 2002 when they opened up Leith Links during the Open week in July when the Open was held at Muirfield present home of the direct descendants of the authors and first players of Leith rules which the Royal and Ancient adopted. They are now recognized throughout the World.

Each year they hold a Hickory Open whereby competitors play using Hickory shafted clubs and play to the original thirteen rules on a replica of the original five hole course.

Gone to the Dogs

Chapter 16

Greyhound racing was started as an experiment to replace hare coursing in 1876 at the Welsh Harp reservoir in Hendon, but it did not catch on.

Owen Patrick Smith invented the mechanical hare in 1912 in an attempt to save wild rabbits and so a sport was born.

Powderhall Stadium opened in 1870 and was used as a venue for different sports. In August 1927 greyhound racing began in Edinburgh attracting crowds of 10,000 and was a favourite night out. William Hendry a motor dealer built a track at Stenhouse on the sight of a former dairy and it opened on 25th. June 1932. With dog racing six nights a week except Tuesdays it was a very lucrative venture however a change in the law in 1935 made gambling illegal. The new regulations only allowed racing on Tuesdays and Saturdays making it impossible to compete with Powderhall so he sold out to the Greyhound Racing Association in 1935. He bought the stadium back in 1950 and rebuilt the grandstands that had been moved to Powderhall. The stadium was used for pony trotting or harness racing and it was also the venue for charity events such as school sports days. The Hendry family sold the stadium to agriculture engineers Andrew Bone in the 1960's.

At Powderhall a disaster happened in August 1948 when a severe flood engulfed the track and Lord Provost Murray had to organize a boat to row across the track to rescue the dogs that were trapped in the kennels. The doors were opened and the dogs swam to safety but out of the 189 in the kennels 20 drowned.

In the post war period the number of people attending race meetings was in excess of 25 million and it became the second largest spectator sport in Britain.

The 1960 Betting and Gaming Act allowed the opening of bookmaker's shops. This put an end to street bookies and punters did not have to go to the track for a wager.

By the 1960's there were 106 meetings a year and to avoid cancellation during inclement weather an electric blanket consisting of eight and a half miles of cable was installed, the first of its kind in Britain. With eight licensed bars the track soon became the best venue in the country.

By the 1980's the number of spectators attending meetings nationwide had dropped to six million with an estimated £650 million in bets. A favourite bet was the Quinella where you had to forecast the 1st. and 2nd dogs in three races.

The Greyhound Racing Association rules are very strict and all dogs racing at their tracks had to be kept in GRA kennels. They were trained by professional trainers at a cost of £2/2s a day plus sixpence (2 ½ p) a day insurance and the dogs underwent regular dope tests. As doping would show up in a test other methods were employed to slow a dog down either to lose a race or get advantageous odds next time out.

The favorite ones were 1lb. mince or a pie fed to them before a race or making them thirsty so they would consume a great deal of water or just over exercise them. Another trick was to put small rubber balls between the pads on the dog's foot making it very difficult to corner causing the dogs to run wide. Dogs running more than half a second slower than their last outing would be scrutinized by the stewards.

Dogs start their racing career aged fifteen months and can race up to between four and six years of age or sooner if they are consistently outside the top four. The champions retire to stud but the fate of the lesser dog is less certain, many are re-homed thanks to greyhound charities but a number are illegally euthanized. It was estimated that in

America 20,000 dogs a year were euthanized before dog charities became involved.

Greyhound racing at tracks (or gaffs as they are known) outside the jurisdiction of the GRA is known as "flapping". These tracks where the facilities are minimal are usually found in small villages.

The first Edinburgh Cup was staged in 1933 and it went on to be one of the top events in the racing calendar. Due to a dispute between the GRA and Shawfield stadium the Scottish Derby was held in 1987and 1988 at Powderhall. The Scottish St. Leger and the Scottish Grand National were also annual events. During a race the dogs can reach a speed of up to 40mph.

In an effort to raise more revenue in 1967 a floodlit golf driving range was opened operating from 10am. to 10pm. On race days, Thursdays and Saturdays, it was 10am.to 6pm. The towers holding the nets were destroyed in the January gales of 1969 and were never replaced and so ended the City's first commercial golf range.

During the 1980's a new grandstand was built costing £400, 000, which was glass fronted to keep out inclement weather. With a bar serving meals and the tote it was a very pleasant way to spend an evening. Unfortunately the building sustained £25,000 damage in a fire in 1987.

Standing on a site measuring 11 acres Powderhall stadium had great development potential. When the GRA decided to sell the kennels to ease their financial burden, local businessman Eddie Ramsay bid £1 million but was unsuccessful. By 1988 their situation had become dire and the GRA accepted a bid from property developer Norrie Rowan, (ex Boroughmuir and Scotland rugby internationalist with 13 caps) of £2 ½ million. He promptly sold it to Coral Racing in 1989 for a profit of £ ½ million. In October 1990 Eddie Ramsay was finally successful in his attempt to buy the stadium with a bid of £3 ½ million to Coral Racing, and despite promises to upgrade the facilities this never materialized. By 1993, complaints about the way the stadium was being run or not being run as the case may be began to be heard. The prize money was not going up and the Bookies were pulling out. At the peak of popularity there had been around twenty bookies working the stadium but now the numbers were down to five or six with each paying £185 a night x 3 nights =£550 a week it was no longer viable for them. Also the crowds were dropping due to an increase in gate money. In September 1993 Ramsay put Powderhall up for sale 2 ½ years after buying it and failing in his promise to keep racing going. In the face of economics this was always going to happen as Ramsay estimated the land was worth 5 times what he had paid for it.

Ramsay used stadium money to pay off other debts and due to missing payments the brewing conglomerate Bass of whom Corals were a subsidy applied for planning permission to build houses and office accommodation. This was granted, and is today the Powderhall housing development and business park. One of the last shows staged there was the International Thrill Show which featured cars and monster trucks performing stunts.

Today there are around twenty eight tracks in Britain where £75 million is wagered.

Powderhall Sprint

Chapter 17

Being a national holiday there was very little in the way of entertainment on New Years Day apart from local football derbys, but one event guaranteed to pull in crowds was a professional foot race.

This was originally known as the Powderhall Sprint, taking its name from the stadium where the event was held for the first one hundred years, it is now known as the New Years Sprint.

The New Years Sprint is the oldest open athletic event in the United Kingdom. Now run over 110 meters it is open to any athlete aged 16 or over, male or female, amateur or professional, contesting prize money worth thousands of pounds. Amateurs are allowed to keep the prize money.

The sprint is not just a race between the fleetest of foot. This event features a handicap system designed to ensure that any runner, no matter what their ability age or sex, has a chance of scooping the large first prize.

The longevity of the event is due to the attraction of champion runners and to on course bookies offering odds and the prospect of the front marker clinging on for victory. That coupled with the determination of the back markers not to be beaten and the fact that it is held at the most inhospitable time of the year are all ingredients that give the sprint an almost mythical air. Run over a course that can have grass three inches long, may be covered in snow or run in a blizzard and held during a horse racing meeting, plus the stories of betting coups in the early years all add to the mystique.

Supporting events include the 90 meters open, 90 meters veterans, 90 meters youths and the 110 meters back markers invitational handicap.

Youth events which also carry cash prizes are open to boys and girls aged between 10-16.

Staged at Powderhall Stadium from 1870 until 1971 when the event was moved to Meadowbank Stadium and then in 2000 moved to its present home at Musselburgh race course.

The 123rd staging of the event in 1993 saw amateur runners competing for the first time due to an agreement between the SGA and the BAAF.

Traditionally held on New Year's Day the event still takes place around that time.

In 1970 George McNeil from Tranent won the centenary event, the last time it was run over 120 yards. His time of 11.61 seconds is still a world record. When the event moved to Meadowbank the distance was changed to 110 metres.

What seems today to be incomprehensible when top class athletes are millionaires, the fact that a child had won a race at a Sunday school picnic and received 1/- (5p) prize money would prevent him /her from competing as an amateur for life.

McNeil who had signed professional forms for Hibernian Football Club but did not make the grade as a footballer was barred from running in what was then an amateur sport so had to compete on the professional circuit. His training regime included having a tractor tyre towed by a rope tied round his waist during his sprints.

In 1972 he beat 1968 Olympic 200 meters gold medalist and world record holder Tommie Smith in a four race series to be crowned World Professional Sprint Champion.

It was Tommie Smith who at the 1968 Olympics in Mexico City gained notoriety along with team mate, Bronze medal winner John Carlos for raising their right arm with clenched fist in the black power salute whilst on the podium after receiving their medals and while the band played the Star Spangled Banner the American National anthem. This resulted in their removal from the American team by Avery Brundage, International Olympic Committee Chairman. The same Avery Brundage who as president of the American Olympic Committee had no objections to the Nazi salutes at the 1936 Berlin Olympics. Ironically this was dominated by black athlete Jesse Owens.

More serious were the death threats made against Smith, Carlos and their families. Smith and Carlos supported by Silver medal winner Australian Peter Norman were protesting at the treatment black Americans received in their own country and their lack of civil rights.

Both these world class athletes, McNeil and Smith suffered at the hands of small minded, creative stifling, bigoted, incompetent bureaucratic people of the mind set which was loathe to make any changes whatsoever even if they were for the good of the sport. This type of thinking which was prevalent at the time would soon be changed bringing amateur sport into the real world.

One of McNeil's biggest triumphs was in 1981 when he was the winner of the Stawell Gift, Australia's most prestigious professional sprint race as well as being the biggest professional sprint race in the world.

In 1975 when the International Track Circuit came to Britain, Chris Brasher who along with Chris Chataway acted as pacemakers when Roger Bannister ran the first sub four minute in 1954. Chris Brasher who went on to become a sporting columnist with the Sunday Observer wrote in his column, "The professionals came to London on Friday and it made me angry, angry because I saw the best British sprinter since McDonald Bailey and knew of the incompetence that meant this talent had been wasted. Angry because I saw one of those rare men who lift sport into the realms of art and knew that his talent was being wasted, angry because such a waste is surely a crime. McNeill is the greatest native born sprinter that I have ever seen in Britain. He has never been allowed to compete for his country or indeed against the best talent in Britain, He has been relegated to the small professional circuit in Scotland where, with the exception of the Powderhall Sprint, he has earned only enough to cover his expenses. On Friday he was with them, battling it out at 90 meters and only tying up with unfamiliar pressure over the last few meters to the tape. McNeill proved that he is in the same class as Hines a dual Olympic Medalist.

George McNeil holds a unique unbeatable record by winning both the Powderhall Sprint and the Stawell Gift in their centenary year.

On his retirement from athletics McNeil became the sprint coach to Heart of Midlothian Football Club, Hibernian Football Club and Livingston where as fitness coach he took them from the 3rd. Division to the Scottish Premier League, as well as winning the League Cup gaining them a place in Europe. He is well known as being a witty and entertaining after dinner speaker.

Jim Bradley was born in 1921 in a single roomed tenement flat in Broughton Street. The second youngest of five children his father deserted the household leaving his mother to bring up the family on her own. Leaving school he joined the LNER railway but due to cutbacks lost his job at the age of seventeen. He joined the army in February 1939 and would serve until the end of the war in 1945. When he returned to Edinburgh in 1946 aged 24 he took up athletics and joined Edinburgh Southern Harriers training at Meadowbank. He soon attracted the eye of George McCrae a top athletic coach who persuaded him to run professionally. In 1947 at Powderhall he won his heat and bookmaker William Murphy offered to sponsor him in preparation for the next year. During 1951 he was the training partner of the famous Australian runner Eric Cummin. When Cummin was beaten in the semi final he was ready to return to Australia but Bradley convinced him to stay and have another attempt in 1952. Cummin did so and became the only Australian to win the event. He won off a tight handicap of two yards on a track covered in snow.

Bradley realizing that his arm action needed improvement began experimenting with different ways to increase his upper body strength and discovered that working with a speedball could produce the desired result. After months of trials he found the best method was six three minute rounds with a minutes break in between.

Opening his own gym he soon attracted runners wishing to improve their times. In 1957 he began working with Ricky Dunbar who would run second in 1962 off a mark of six yards before winning in 1963 off 4 ½ yards. In 1969 George McNeil joined his stable and won in 1970 and ran second in 1971 off scratch. Under Bradley, McNeil broke the World Professional 120 yard record on the way to winning the British professional sprint title.

Between 1962 and 1971 Bradley coached eleven Powderhall sprint finalists including five winners. Emigrating to Australia in 1972 he began fitness coaching to Australian Rules football teams before running his own sporting goods stores.

Bradley made a return to athletic coaching in 1988 at the age of sixty seven. Within two years his stable of runners were virtually unbeatable with many of his runners multiple finalists. On New Year's Day 1990 he set a record with the first and second in two of Australia's most prestigious races and in January of that year at the Rye Gift Carnival his runners took the first four places. He also has the distinction of having trained the first and second in both the New Year's Sprint and the Stawell Gift. A record that will never be broken. Apart from speedball and body weight exercises Bradley advocated a diet of steak and chips with plenty of fruit and vegetables.

One of his proteges Wilson Young using Jim Bradley's speedball method trained Alan Wells winner of the 100 metres Gold Medal at the Moscow Olympics in 1980.

Motor Racing, Speedway

Chapter 18

Motor racing came to the capital with the opening of the Ingliston Racing Circuit in 1965, it proved to be very popular with names such as Stirling Moss, Jim Clark, Jackie Stewart and David Coultart taking part in races, Due to lack of investment and increased competition from Knockhill Racing Circuit it became unviable and closed in 1995. Part of the track is still used as a driving experience in super cars.

From a back street lock-up to international fame rose the race team Ecurie Ecosse.

The name Ecurie Ecosse translates from the French as Scotland Stable.

Founded in 1951 by businessman and avid amateur racing driver David Murray and his mechanic Walter "Wilkie" Wilkinson in a mews garage in Merchiston their stable won back to back Le Mans 24 hour endurance race in 1956 & 57. Drivers included Ron Flockart, Innes Ireland, Jimmy Stewart and his brother 3 times formula one champion Sir Jackie Stewart. The cars were D type Jaguars.

The team also raced in three Formula One races in 1952-3-4. Ecurie Ecosse's cars were always distinctive in their flag blue metallic paint. Car enthusiast Dick Skipworth had a collection of their cars including the car transporter which sold at Bonhams for £8.8 million, the car transporter fetched a record £1.8 million a world record for a historical commercial vehicle the transporter and two cars going to America after a bidding war lasting almost half an hour.

The team disbanded in 1972 then reformed in 1982 and over the years ownership has changed hands but the team still win events on the European circuit.

Racing on two wheels has proved more enduring but no longer has a presence in the city however the fan base of Edinburgh Monarchs remains strong.

Speedway in Britain was imported from Australia in 1928, where it was very popular, and was introduced at Marine Gardens a pleasure complex in Portobello and now a bus garage. It ran until 1931 pulling in big crowds sometimes as many as 20,000. Racing was resumed in 1938 but only for two seasons, as in 1940 all speedway in Britain was banned because of the war.

At this time the riders wore a thistle on their breastplate, some of the riders were, Papa Forsythe who was known as a great character, a world class American "Sprouts" Elder, Norrie Isbester, Drew McQueen and George McKenzie who is also credited with introducing roller skating to Marine Gardens after seeing it in Manchester.

Marine Gardens was not available after the war so promoter Johnny Hoskins, who was known as the father of Speedway, chartered a light plane and flew over the city to identify possible venues.

The one chosen was Leith Athletic Football Club ground at Old Meadowbank (now the site of the Meadowbank Stadium at London Road) and Speedway as we know it today was born.

The team was named the Monarchs and the first captain was an Australian named Bill Maddern, fellow Aussie Clem Mitchell was also in the team as was New Zealander Dick Campbell a former wall of death rider.

Finishing bottom of division 2 in their first season the track was altered making the corners narrower to make the racing better, legend has it that the football club did not want the track altered but the speedway people sneaked in at night and altered it anyway.

In 1949 Clem Mitchell told of a young man from Adelaide who was doing well in Australia named Jack Young and he was duly signed, a signing that would transform the sport. In his first meeting he won all four of his races and three days later was taken into hospital to have his appendix removed and so missed the next few meetings but still had a successful season. In 1950 he reached the final of the World Championship and won it in 1951 while still riding in the second division. This was to become the golden age of the Monarchs with crowds of 20.-25,000 regularly turning out to watch and wonder at his skill and he was making celebrity appearances in the city promoting the sport.

It was inevitable that top class teams would try to sign him and in 1952 he was transferred to West Ham for a world record fee of £3,750, he could not be replaced and the team suffered after his departure. The coming of television coupled with the introduction of entertainment tax at 60% of gate receipts saw the sport go into a decline and in July 1954 the Monarchs finished. Their farewell meeting was attended by a 7,000 crowd. It was indeed a sad day for the fans many of whom attended as a family.

Stock car racing was introduced but could not capture the fans imagination and did not last long.

In 1959 a young American student named Ian Hart gained permission to stage a speedway meeting in aid of the Edinburgh University Students charity appeal and he repeated the meeting the following year.

Ian Hoskins, son of the legendary Johnny decided to reintroduce the Monarchs and so in 1960 the Monarchs returned to Old Meadowbank in the Provincial league and crowds of 5-10,000 came along on a regular basis, indeed it was a popular Saturday night out.

Hoskins discovered two Fife farmers, brothers Doug and Willie Templeton who were riding on grass tracks at fairs and farmers shows, and signed them over the phone. George Hunter a talented but temperamental rider was also in the team as was the veteran Dick Campbell.

The Monarchs had their ups and downs during this period and when Scottish Television decided to broadcast meetings the Monarchs could not have anticipated the outcome. Ross Campbell, four year old son of Dick Campbell and team mascot was seen by police chiefs riding his miniature bike and leading the team in the introductory parade and was duly ordered to stop for "safety reasons".

In 1963 Monarchs put their unbeaten run on the line with a visit from Belle Vue on Friday 20th September. In the Belle Vue team was two times World Champion "The Wizard of Balance" Peter Craven. Monarchs held a four point lead going into heat ten which would see George Hunter who was their best rider that year meet Peter Craven for the first time, Hunter led all the way only to be pipped by Craven for a shared race. They met again in heat twelve and once again Hunter took the lead but tragedy struck in the second lap when Hunter fell on the first bend, Craven following close behind attempting to avoid the fallen Hunter clipped his wheel and crashed into the safety fence, taken to hospital with serious head injuries he died on Tuesday 24th September. This was the worst single blow the world of speedway had suffered and although no blame was attached to him the tragedy would haunt Hunter for the rest of his life.

In an ill advised attempt to make the sport more exciting it was decided to hold meetings using modified bikes in Murrayfield ice rink but ice racing never caught the imagination of the true speedway supporter so the idea was quickly discarded.

A new era for speedway began in 1965 when the warring Provincial League and the National League settled their differences and became the British League this meant that all the top teams and riders would visit Old Meadowbank. In 1967 when Edinburgh was awarded the Commonwealth Games for 1970 a new stadium was required and Old Meadowbank was chosen. Monarchs were evicted and were not promised a home in the new stadium as the government of the day would not put money into a stadium that would hold professional sports. Ironical when you think that athletic stars are paid a lot of money some astronomical amounts helping them achieve millionaire status, and so the final league meeting took place against Sheffield on the 30th. September 1967 and with it the end came for one of the best tracks in the country.

With the search on for a new home and none available in Edinburgh Ian Hoskins extended his search further afield finally deciding on Albion Rovers football ground at Cliftonhill in Coatbridge but this was not long term and in the close season it was announced that the Monarchs license had been sold to Wembley and the final meeting at Coatbridge took place on 11th. October1970.

In 1976 the Greyhound Racing Association sought permission to hold speedway meetings at Powderhall Stadium after noise tests had been conducted and numerous council meetings permission was granted and work started on construction of the track.

With new promoter Mike Parker in charge the new season started on 15th. April 1977 with a challenge match against Berwick Bandits.

Financial problems within the club came to a head in January 1991. A meeting was held at Powderhall to discuss the difficulties facing the club, the response from the gathered supporters was a pledge of £16,000 so racing was guaranteed for the 1991 season. The hero of the hour was Mike Hunter who organized the meeting and formed a fighting fund "The Friends of Edinburgh Speedway" which still exists today.

The G.R.A. sold out to local nightclub owner Eddie Ramsey on the promise that speedway and greyhound racing would continue at the track, but Ramsey had other ideas and 1995 would be the last year for both at this friendly little stadium as Ramsey sold out to developers and the area is now a housing estate.

Monarchs made an application in 1996 to hold meetings at Armadale 20 miles to the west of the Capital but permission was refused.

With Glasgow Tigers in trouble and unable to raise a team and owning Shawfield Stadium and Monarchs with a team but no track an amalgamation seemed the logical step giving both sets of supporters the chance to watch racing, but the amalgamation was a disaster. What was not taken into account was the inherent rivalry between the two cities with only 250-300 supporters traveling from Edinburgh and the Tigers faithful refusing to watch what was basically an Edinburgh team crowd figures were below break even.

An appeal against the refusal to their application to hold meetings at Armadale went in Monarchs favour and at last the team had a permanent home.

In 1997 two leagues were formed the Elite League and the Premier League, Monarchs entered the Premier League. Over the years Monarchs have won many honours, twice becoming Premier League champions in 2003 and 2008. Premier Trophy winners 2008, Scottish Cup winners 21 times including an impressive 8 consecutive from 1999-2007 and a World Champion in Jack Young in 1951.

Wrestling

Chapter 19

The Eldorado Stadium and Ballroom in Mill Lane was the home for many years to boxing matches and "all in" wrestling bouts, Hugh McGourty was the owner.

Many of the big names of the dance band era played the venue the resident being the legendary Tommy Sampson the leader of a twenty strong orchestra who became one of the "big five" bands during the big band era of the late forties and fifties. Many a Leith couple met in the ballroom.

In the 1950-60's all in wrestling was very popular thanks in part to being televised on a Saturday afternoon. Many women were among the spectators and were always very vociferous in their praise of their favourites or derision for the villains often attacking them with handbags or umbrellas on their way back to the dressing room, all in all a rowdy night. The only seating was at ringside everywhere else it was standing. Max Crabtree the promoter was one of three wrestling brothers the other two being Brian and Shirley, Brian retired through injury but continued in the sport as a referee known for his flamboyant dress. Instead of the traditional white shirt he sported a black and red spangly jacket. Older brother Shirley would go on to fight under the name "Big Daddy" and instead of wearing a dressing gown would sport a coloured spangly cape with matching top hat. Max an independent promoter was responsible for staging wrestling bouts featuring the big names from England such as "Iron man" Steve Logan, Mick McManus and his arch rival Jackie "Mr T.V" Pallo,

Among the favourites were Alan Dennison, Les Kellet, "the Clown Prince" and "Black Butcher" Johnston, famous for his mule kicks. Billy Two Rivers would enter the ring wearing a Red Indian headdress and do a war dance before the contest and Andy Robbins with his tame bear called Hercules. There would always be a big name contest or a title challenge ensuring it was a full house every Tuesday. It was a common belief that the programme would always end at 9.40 so allowing fans to get a drink before the pubs closed at 10pm.

The regulars had their favourites and chaos broke out if they were beaten. On one occasion in a tag match the Black Diamonds beat local favourites Alan Dennison and Jim Breaks, the crowd went berserk and chased the winners out of the stadium and along Great Junction Street.

One of the all time greats was Lightweight George Kidd from Dundee the greatest technical wrestler of his time who was undisputed World Champion for twenty six years and made forty nine defenses of his title before retiring undefeated.

His matches were always on in the first half of the bill so allowing him to catch a train back to Dundee.

He fought in the Albert Hall in London in front of Prince Phillip.

His favourite trick was to roll up into a ball leaving his opponent nothing to hold onto; he partnered DJ Jimmy Saville in tag team contests.

Jimmy Saville took up wrestling to raise money for charity and was trained by Les Kellet, he had one hundred and seven bouts losing the first thirty five, (how's about that then).

Everyone knew that the fights were fixed, the villains would wind the crowd up into a frenzy with very obvious breaking of the rules before the hero made a spectacular recovery to win, but accidents did happen. Masambula, always very popular with the crowd, entered the ring wearing a headdress of a leopard skin, During the contest when he got into difficulties he would do a tribal dance and a witch doctor routine to put a spell on his opponent.

During a contest in Derby he was thrown against the corner post where the padding was not secured and injured his spine, collapsing to the floor. He was body slammed by his unaware opponent as he lay helpless, the crowd unaware of the extent of his injury were screaming for him to get back on his feet. It was only when he was stretchered out of the ring that they realized he was not faking. He spent the rest of his life in a wheelchair.

With the demise of ballroom dancing and wrestling the venue was turned into a skateboarding arena before it was destroyed by fire on 15th. July 1984.

Cinemas closing dates

Alhambra Leith Walk	1914-1958
Astoria Manse Road	1930-1974
Blue Halls (Beverley) Lauriston Street	1930-1959
Bungalow (Victory)Bath Street	1914-1956
Caley Lothian Road	1923-1984
Cameo (Kings)Home Street	1914-
Capital Manderson Street	1928-1961
Carlton Piershill	1935-1959
Central (George)Portobello High Street	1915-1942
County (George) Bath Street	1939-1954
County (Rio) Wauchope Avenue	1950-1963
Dominion Newbattle Terrace	1938
Eastway (Picturedrome) Easter Road	1943-1961
Embassy Boswall Parkway	1937-1964
Gaumont (Rutland) Canning Street	1950-1963
Grand St. Stephens Street	1920-1960
Jacey (Monsiegneur) Princes Street	1964-1973
Lyceum Slateford Road	1926-1960
La Scala (Classic) Nicholson Street	1912-1980's
New Palace High Street	1929-1956
New Tivoli (Tivoli) Gorgie Road	1934- 1973
New Victoria (Odeon) Nicholson Street	1930 -2003
Palace Constitution Street	1913-1966
Palace Princes Street	1913-1955
Playhouse Greenside Place	1929-1973
Poole's Roxy Gorgie Road	1937-1963
Poole's Synod Hall	1928-1965
Regal (ABC Odeon) Lothian Road	1938-
Regent Abbeymount	1937-1970
Ritz Rodney Street	1929-1983
The Salon Baxters Place	1913-1974
Savoy (Tudor) St.Bernards Row	1925-1966
Scotia (Haymarket) Dalry Road	1912-1964
State Great Junction Street	1938-1972